AN INVESTIGATION OF THE MEASUREMENT OF POVERTY IN IRELAND

Colin Menton

IPA

INSTITUTE OF PUBLIC
ADMINISTRATION
50 Years
CELEBRATING PUBLIC SERVICE
1957 – 2007

First published in 2007
by the Institute of Public Administration
57–61 Lansdowne Road
Dublin 4
Ireland

www.ipa.ie

ISBN: 978-1-904541-61-5

British Library cataloguing-in-publication data
A catalogue record for this book is available from the British Library

Cover design by Alice Campbell, Dublin
Typeset by Computertype, Dublin
Printed in England by Cromwell Press, Trowbridge, Wiltshire

Contents

Figures

Tables

Preface

This book is based on a thesis entitled 'An Investigation of Key Difficulties Associated with the Measurement of Poverty in an Irish Context', which was undertaken for the Masters in Economic Science (Policy Analysis) programme. An abridged version of the original text is presented here for publication as a book. Although there have been a number of relevant developments since the research was completed in 2006, it is important to point out that the thrust of the analysis remains current. Notable developments include publication of 2005 EU-SILC data, measures introduced in Budget 2007, the publication by the ESRI of proposals for revising the consistent poverty measure and the publication of the National Action Plan for Social Inclusion 2007–2016 which adopts a poverty-reducing target framed around the revised definition of consistent poverty. A number of minor updates have been made to the original text to reflect some of these developments. Others, however, have not been taken on board as to do so would require a fundamental reworking of the research.

I would like, in particular, to acknowledge the invaluable insight and assistance of Dr Micheál L. Collins in helping to bring the thesis underlying this work to fruition. I am also grateful to Dr Michael Mulreany and the Institute of Public Administration for their support and encouragement. I would like to acknowledge the support and help of work colleagues and the assistance provided by the Central Statistics Office in providing a range of data to support the analysis. Finally, I would like to thank Jennifer Armstrong for the invaluable assistance she provided in terms of editing the material for publication.

Abbreviations

AHC	After housing costs
BHC	Before housing costs
CIÉ	Córas Iompair Éireann
CORI	Conference of Religious of Ireland
CPA	Combat Poverty Agency
CSO	Central Statistics Office
DWP	Department of Work and Pensions (UK)
ECHP	European Community Household Panel (survey)
EQLS	European Quality of Life Survey
ESB	Electricity Supply Board
ESRI	Economic and Social Research Institute
EU	European Union
EUROMOD	Europe-wide tax-benefit model
EU-SILC	EU Survey on Income and Living Conditions
GDP	Gross domestic product
GNP	Gross national product
HBAI	Households below average income
HBS	Household Budget Survey
INOU	Irish National Organisation of the Unemployed
IR	Imputed rent
LCA	Low cost but acceptable (budget standard)
LIIS	Living in Ireland Survey
MABS	Money Advice and Budgeting Service
MBA	Modest but adequate (budget standard)
MIQ	Minimum income question
NAPS	National Anti-Poverty Strategy
NAPinclusion	National Action Plan for Social Inclusion
NAPsincl	National Action Plan against Poverty and Social Exclusion
NESC	National Economic and Social Council
NESF	National Economic and Social Forum
OECD	Organisation for Economic Co-operation and Development
PPP	Purchasing power parity

PPS	Purchasing power standard
PSE	Poverty and Social Exclusion (survey)
SWITCH	Simulating welfare and income tax change (model)
UN	United Nations
UNICEF	United Nations International Children's Emergency Fund

1

Introduction

There is a growing unease in Ireland with the present approach to the measurement of poverty and consequently with the poverty targets framed around such measures. A number of factors have contributed to this sense of unease. For example, a period of unprecedented economic growth has been accompanied by rising rates of poverty. Expenditure on social provision and public services has significantly increased, yet statistics reveal increasing proportions of vulnerable groups falling below the poverty line. The ESRI surveys which ran from 1994 to 2001 showed consistent poverty to be falling steadily to 4.1 per cent, however the EU-SILC survey introduced in 2003 found the consistent poverty rate to be much higher at 8.8 per cent. Such contradictions undermine the credibility of current poverty measures.

The purpose of this work is to investigate some of the main difficulties associated with the systems used to measure poverty in Ireland and to suggest how such difficulties might be overcome. There are a number of challenges associated with the measurement of poverty: poor levels of understanding about how and why we measure poverty, the limitations and complexity of the measures themselves and the sheer volume of international academic research, literature, policy documents and reports on issues relating to poverty measurement.

This study has two key objectives. The first is to try to bridge the gap that exists between the policy-making process and the vast body of research, studies and reports by providing a clear explanation, analysis and synthesis of the difficulties associated with the measurement of poverty in an Irish context. The second is to explore what scope there is to overcome these difficulties. This analysis is intended to contribute to the search for a robust, stable and reliable system of measurement to underpin an effective evidence-based approach to policy and decision-making on poverty and social inclusion issues.

The analysis begins with an examination in Chapter 2 of how poverty is defined and of the main approaches taken to the measurement of poverty, identifying their principal strengths and weaknesses.

Turning to the Irish context, Chapter 3 outlines the influences on policy, the main sources of poverty-related data and the recent trends in respect of the two headline poverty measures used in Ireland: relative income poverty and consistent poverty.

Chapters 4 to 9 offer in-depth explorations of six key difficulties associated with the measurement of poverty in Ireland:

1. The paradox of high rates of economic growth being accompanied by rising poverty rates and the impact this has on the credibility of measures based on relative income.
2. The misleading impressions given by comparisons of relative income poverty rates across European countries.
3. The ability of income-based poverty measures to offer a fair reflection of the standard of living of certain groups in society such as those dependent on social welfare.
4. The fact that relative income poverty measures in Ireland fail to take account of housing costs or benefits.
5. The adequacy of the consistent poverty measure in reflecting poverty in contemporary Ireland.
6. The potential for confusion among policy-makers and the public at large arising from the way that poverty is measured and how poverty statistics are presented and communicated.

Each chapter explains and justifies the difficulty under consideration, discusses possible ways of addressing the issue and reaches a set of conclusions and implications.

Finally, Chapter 10 attempts to knit together the conclusions reached and sets forth a number of overall conclusions of relevance to future considerations and discussions on the measurement of poverty.

2

The Conceptualisation and Measurement of Poverty

This chapter provides the academic context for an analysis of the issues and problems associated with poverty measurement.

Defining poverty

Our approaches to poverty and poverty measurement stem from the way in which poverty is conceptualised. However, there is no single 'society-approved' definition of poverty (Piachaud, 1987) and different definitions can produce dramatically different rates of poverty.

Historical definitions of poverty are rooted in the 'absolute' view, where the concern is with narrow concepts of income and the maintenance of physical efficiency. Absolute poverty is concerned with basic nutritional needs, the ability to escape avoidable disease, the availability of shelter and clothing etc. Cantillon (2000) explains that this approach stems from a time when it was natural to think in subsistence terms. For Tovey *et al.* (1996), 'an absolute view of poverty assumes that it is possible to determine in some "scientific" or "value-free" way what counts as a minimal acceptable standard of living'. Poverty arises through failure to meet this standard. In practice, this tends to be the most basic needs for subsistence and physical survival, without, as Gordon (2000) points out, reference to social context or norms.

The pioneering work of Rowntree in York at the turn of the twentieth century is an example of an absolutist approach to the measurement of poverty. Rowntree (1901) suggested that those whose total earnings were insufficient to obtain the minimum necessaries for the maintenance of merely physical efficiency were experiencing what he termed as 'primary poverty'. A poverty line was constructed based on the cost of the food required to meet average nutritional needs for a person or family and minimum costs for clothing, fuel and household sundry needs according to family size. The idea was that it would be impossible to argue that people with income below the primary poverty line could avoid 'want

3

or squalor', however efficiently they managed their resources (Hills, 2004).

Townsend (1974) observes that, for much of the twentieth century, nearly all subsequent studies were influenced deeply by Rowntree's application of the concept of subsistence. For instance, the landmark Beveridge Report of 1942, which served as a blueprint for the modern British welfare state, drew on Rowntree's definition of poverty and advocated a subsistence standard as the right basis for paying benefits in a social security scheme designed to abolish want. However, as societies develop, living standards diverge and become more complex and subsistence is taken more or less for granted.

In such developed societies, definitions of poverty tend to evolve from an absolute to a relative conception. The relative concept of poverty incorporates a recognition of the way in which the general standard of living in a society influences what is regarded as a minimum standard of subsistence in that society. In other words 'it is defined in relation to the general level of prosperity in a country or population group at a given point in time' (Atkinson *et al.*, 2002).

Poverty, according to the relative definition, can have a different meaning for different societies. Societies have differing levels of expectations, imposed by their particular occupational, economic and educational systems, and generate varying levels of want through the way they are organised and their individual customs. What is regarded as adequate by a society will change over time and will differ across societies.

At European level, a relative definition of poverty was adopted by the Council of Europe in 1975 (Commission of the European Communities, 1981). Within this definition those regarded as being in poverty include 'individuals or families whose resources are so small as to exclude them from the minimum accepted way of life of the Member State in which they live'. The word 'resources' was subsequently defined as encompassing goods, cash income and public and private services.

The EU expanded its relative definition of poverty in 1984 to state that 'the poor shall be taken to mean persons, families and groups of persons whose resources (material, cultural and social) are so limited as to exclude them from the minimum acceptable way of life in the Member State in which they live' (EEC, 1984). UNICEF (2000) suggests that the relative definition of poverty is the most commonly used definition in the industrialised world, but points out that when it is operationalised it amounts to 'those whose incomes fall below half of the average income for the nation in which they live'. Income-based poverty lines can be seen as focusing wholly on the 'resources' element of the definition. Here poverty is conceptualised in similar terms to inequality with the emphasis on inequalities in the income distribution.

Poverty in developing countries, however, continues to be conceptualised in absolutist terms by international organisations. For example, in 1991, the World Bank defined a poverty line for 'poor' countries as $1 a day per person in 1985 prices. Cantillon (2000) holds that poverty and inequality are two distinct concepts. In that even if there is no poverty, in the sense that no one would be so far below the general standard of living as to be excluded from participation in the ordinary life of that society, there could still be substantial inequality in the distribution of income between the wealthy and the rest of society. Atkinson *et al.* (2002) reinforce this point, arguing that the relative nature of poverty should not be overemphasised or exaggerated to the extent that confusion arises between the notions of poverty and income inequality. This would serve to undermine the credibility of the poverty standard. Assigning the term 'poor' to those in the bottom quintile of the income distribution would make no sense because this would mean that 20 per cent of the population, by definition, would always be in poverty.

Townsend and Gordon (2002) argue that there are weaknesses associated with definitions that involve numbers of people with incomes below an arbitrary percentage of the average. While it is politically convenient to have one benchmark that is 'fairly easy to estimate in several countries', such measures cannot be considered 'scientifically based' given that they are not derived using independent criteria of deprivation or disadvantage, the needs of individuals or any agreed definition of what it is to be poor. As Townsend noted in 1974, the criterion of cash income is inadequate. There are groups in the population with considerable income-in-kind such as farmers and small-holders. There are people with small cash incomes but considerable assets that elevate their standards of living. This calls for a wider concept of 'resources' to replace income in the study of poverty and inequality, while at the same time 'style of living' should replace 'consumption' in determining what levels in the ranking of resources should be regarded as constituting deprivation.

During the 1970s Townsend developed the concept of 'relative deprivation', which proposed that below a certain income level – a threshold of deprivation – the number of items people lacked accelerated and that this could be used to measure poverty 'objectively'. In what was to become an influential definition of poverty, Townsend (1974) argued that 'individuals, families and groups in the population can be said to be in poverty when they lack the resources to obtain the types of diets, participate in the activities and have the living conditions and amenities which are customary, or are at least widely encouraged or approved, in the societies to which they belong'.

Today, relative deprivation is usually the preferred measure because it examines deprivation subject to a household's social and economic context. This approach reflects the multi-dimensional nature of poverty in terms of inadequate income, limited education, poor employment prospects, difficult neighbourhood conditions and so on. Individuals experiencing such cumulative deprivation could be said to be suffering from non-participation in various important parts of life. Hence, the relative definition of poverty introduces a number of related concepts such as 'marginalisation', 'deprivation' and 'social exclusion'.

As Tovey *et al.* (1996) point out, 'people who are poor in material terms are often also poor in social terms (they are unable to meet the obligations or expectations that are associated with normal social relationships in their society), and often also in political terms (they are excluded from participation in decision making within their society)'. It is now widely accepted that in seeking to eliminate poverty in a comprehensive way, there needs to be an emphasis on tackling this kind of social exclusion and marginalisation.

At the Copenhagen World Summit on Social Development in 1995, 117 countries adopted a two-tiered approach to the definition of poverty, consisting of an absolute definition and an overall definition. Absolute poverty was defined as:

A condition characterised by severe deprivation of basic human needs, including food, safe drinking water, sanitation facilities, health, shelter, education and information. It depends not only on income but also on access to services.

Overall poverty, which could take various forms, was defined as:

Lack of income and productive resources to ensure sustainable livelihoods; hunger and malnutrition; ill health; limited or lack of access to education and other basic services; increased morbidity and mortality from illness; homelessness and inadequate housing; unsafe environments and social discrimination and exclusion. It is also characterised by lack of participation in decision-making and in civil, social and cultural life.

Summit participants committed to eradicate absolute poverty, to reduce overall poverty and to draw up national poverty-alleviation plans. Ireland was one of the first countries to produce a National Anti-Poverty Strategy (NAPS) in response to these commitments. Launched in 1997, the NAPS included the following definition of poverty, which is framed in relative terms and, significantly, encompasses the concept of social exclusion:

People are living in poverty if their income and resources (material, cultural and social) are so inadequate as to preclude them from having a standard of living which is regarded as acceptable by Irish society generally. As a result of inadequate income and resources people may be excluded and marginalised from participating in activities which are considered the norm for other people in society.

In conclusion, the conceptualisation of poverty has evolved from absolutist definitions towards a relative conceptualisation, latterly encompassing the notion of relative deprivation and the allied terms of marginalisation and social exclusion. Defining poverty, as Halleröd *et al.* (1997) note, is about finding those 'indicators which separate people suffering from multiple deprivation and hardship from people who live more or less ordinary but not necessarily totally unproblematic lives'.

Measuring poverty

Atkinson (1987) is of the view that there is likely to be a diversity of judgements affecting all aspects of measuring poverty and that this should be recognised in the procedures adopted. A consequence of this realisation is that measures will produce 'less all-embracing answers' which may only allow us to make broad comparisons rather than to achieve a precise measurement of difference. Such comparisons may lead only to a partial, as opposed to a complete, ordering. For Atkinson, however, it is important to recognise that such partial answers are better than no answer at all. This theme is central to the discussion of the approaches to poverty measurement which follows. For the purposes of analysis, the main approaches taken to the measurement of poverty are grouped into three categories: financial poverty measures, non-monetary/deprivation measures and combined income and deprivation measures.

1. Measures of financial poverty

Financial poverty indicators are based on income or expenditure, or a combination of both. Atkinson *et al.* (2002) suggest that financial indicators of poverty are sufficient where the concern is with a 'rights' concept of poverty in terms of a right to the minimum level of resources required to facilitate full participation by an individual in a particular society at a particular time.

Income

Definitions of poverty at both national and EU level are couched in terms of the level of resources required to have a standard of living that is considered the norm for that society. In trying to capture or measure these 'resources' most emphasis has been placed on income. Indeed, Eurostat, in recent years, has tended to use income as the key indicator of financial poverty. One of the main reasons for this is that income data is now available on a harmonised basis across the EU.

Economists differ over how income should be defined. Nevertheless, many agree with Henry Simons' 1938 definition, that income should be regarded as 'the value of rights to which a person might exercise in consumption without altering the value of his assets' (cited in Atkinson, 1974). That is, the market value of all goods consumed plus the increase in the value of the person's wealth during the period in question.

Cantillon (2000) distinguishes three types of income. The first and most common is 'direct' or 'market' income. This includes earned income from wages/salaries and self-employment and other cash income from private sources (e.g. property, pensions, alimony or child support). The second is 'gross' income, which is derived by adding to direct or market income all social transfer payments received. This might include family allowances, unemployment benefits and welfare benefits. Finally, 'disposable' income, which is most commonly used in welfare analysis, is calculated by deducting employee tax and employee and employer social insurance contributions from 'gross' income. Nolan *et al.* (2000) draw attention to the fact that disposable income is not necessarily equal to 'take-home pay', which will be net of a range of other deductions including pension contributions, trade union subscriptions, health insurance contributions and any other deductions made by the employer at source.

It is also worth noting that there are differences between how income is defined in Ireland and at EU level. The EU definition does not include income from private pensions. Also under the EU definition, all contributions to pension plans, except private pension plans, are deducted from gross income when calculating disposable income. Under the national definition of income, no pension contributions of any kind are deducted from gross income.

Nolan and Smeeding (2004) differentiate between earnings and income. Earnings refers to persons, and income refers to households. Income pools the earnings of household members, taxes, transfers, pensions and capital income. Each of these items tends to result in the distribution of household income being very different from the distribution of individual or household earnings. The NESC (2005b) concedes that examining the impact of each of these income sources on the overall distribution of household income presents difficulties.

Individual income is derived through tax and social security records. Household income is obtained through household surveys. Household surveys collect a wide range of income-related data from various sources including: employee earnings, self-employment, farming, secondary jobs, casual employment, state training or work experience schemes, social welfare transfers by scheme, child benefit, the renting of land or property, interest or dividends, retirement pensions, pensions from abroad, annuities, covenants or trusts, sick pay from an employer, trade union strike or sick pay, private or charitable maintenance from outside the household, and educational grants (Nolan *et al.*, 2000).

Atkinson (1974) explores a number of conceptual problems which arise in terms of income measurement. For example, one issue relates to the definition of the basic unit for which information should be analysed. There are three options: the individual, the nuclear family or the household. The choice depends on the degree to which a group of persons share their income.

Another problem arises in relation to the choice of time period over which resources should be measured. The extremes present difficulties. Weekly income is very sensitive to chance fluctuations. For example, the week in question could be the one week an individual does not work overtime or could be the week in which an annual bonus is received. The other extreme would involve the aggregation of a person's income over their entire lifetime. A 'lifetime income' approach, however, is not very relevant when the concern is with a person's current predicament. An old person could have had high income over their working career but be living in poverty now. Atkinson *et al.* (2002) recommend a hybrid approach called 'current modified income'. This consists of annualised current regular income components (wages, social welfare and/or pensions multiplied by twelve if paid monthly). For irregular income components (e.g. self-employment income, annual bonuses and so on), figures for the most recent and appropriate period should be used.

A related issue concerns timing in terms of the availability of data. Data on the distribution of household income lags behind the data available on market earnings and information on tax and transfer changes arising from the most recent budget decisions.

One of the key difficulties associated with income measurement relates to the accuracy of income data. There are two aspects to this. The first relates to the coverage of household surveys, which do not capture all income, for example capital gains. The second relates to the reliability of the income figures provided by those surveyed. There are particular problems in relation to self-employment and income from property. Reliability is further undermined by the tendency for low response rates from those at the top of the income range. The combination of all of these factors means that income overall tends to be understated.

Another limitation relates to the fact that cash income does not capture everything about an individual's living standards. People have different needs or may have sources of income not counted by conventional measures. Gordon *et al.* (2000b) list a range of items that the measurement of income fails to take into account. These include personal and capital assets, fringe benefits, occupational welfare, income-in-kind, the value of free or subsidised services and the quality of the environment. The 2001 report of the Benchmarking and Indexation Group also drew attention to shortcomings of disposable income as currently defined, highlighting as particularly important the fact that no account is taken of housing costs.

Equivalence scales
The household is commonly adopted as the 'income-sharing unit' with the assumption made that income is equally distributed among all household members, providing them with equal standards of living. Eurostat (1999) defines a household as comprising 'either one person living alone or a group of persons, not necessarily related, living at the same address with common housekeeping – i.e. sharing a meal on most days or sharing a living or sitting room'.

It is logical that a constant level of income will generate different standards of living for those in a large versus a small household, or one comprising adults rather than mostly children. Therefore income has to be adjusted for the differing needs associated with differing household size and composition. While it would be possible to calculate income on a per capita basis, this would not reflect the differing needs within households and the economies of scale in terms of cost savings achieved when two or more people live together.

Household income can be adjusted to reflect these considerations using an 'equivalence scale'. The equivalence scale permits the calculation of the number of 'equivalent adults' in the household. Actual household income is then divided by the number of equivalent adults in the household (or 'equivalent household size') to yield a figure for 'equivalised income'. Weighting each household by the number of persons it contains allows us to examine the distribution of income among persons.

Various methods have been used to calculate equivalence scales (each producing different results) and a large number of such scales are used within and across countries. There is no consensus around which scales or methodologies for estimating them are most appropriate. Atkinson (1998) argues that the appropriate scale may vary from country to country depending on the extent of fixed household costs such as housing, heating and property taxes. Where such costs are low, then standard of living considerations may point to a scale closer to per capita than is the case where fixed costs are higher.

Nolan *et al.* (2000) highlight five different equivalence scales that are commonly used in the analysis of poverty and income distribution in Ireland, Europe and internationally. They also analyse how each impacts on the Irish income distribution. These five scales are as follows:

1. The Irish 'national' scale assigns a value of 1 to the first adult – the household head, 0.66 to each subsequent adult (aged 14 years and over) and 0.33 to each child (0 to 13 years). This scale was derived from the relationships implicit in social welfare payment rates as they operated in 1987. For a household of two adults and two children this scale yields an equivalised household size of 2.32.
2. The UK scale assigns a value of 1 to the first adult, 0.6 to each subsequent adult and 0.4 to each child in the household. Applied to the example of a household of two adults and two children this scale yields an equivalised household size of 2.4.
3. The OECD scale assigns a value of 1 to the first adult, 0.7 to each subsequent adult and 0.5 to each child. In the example of a household of two adults and two children this scale yields an equivalised household size of 2.7.
4. A 'modified' OECD scale was devised as a result of the OECD scale's relative generosity to large families. It assigns a value of 1 to the household head, 0.5 to each subsequent adult and 0.3 to each child (under 14 years). The impact of this modification can be seen when applied to the example of a household with two adults and two children. Now the equivalised household size is 2.1.
5. The final scale involves using the square root of household size, without distinguishing between adults and children. In a household of four persons (two adults and two children) this yields an equivalent household size of 2.

Overall, Nolan *et al.* conclude that the shape of the income distribution is very similar across all five scales. However, Atkinson *et al.* (2002) point out that the choice of equivalence scale impacts directly on the number of poor, especially among large households and will affect the composition of the poor population.

Equivalence scales fail to take into account those factors other than size and composition that cause households to vary and that affect the demands on their income. These include the ages of the adults and children in the household and their health status. How does one capture the implications of a chronic disability on needs? Nolan (2002) instances work-related expenses such as transport and childcare as factors affecting the net income available to support living standards. Another factor is regional price variations. Even when two households have the same equivalised income, it is a reality that the purchasing power of that income might be greater for one household than for the other depending on their geographic location. Townsend (1979) also observes that 'equivalence' appears to vary proportionately at different income levels, citing one study which showed that 'richer' families found children relatively more costly than 'poorer' families.

Cantillon (2000) points to studies which show that resources are not always shared equally among the members of the household with the result that some members of the household are worse off than others or that there is 'hidden poverty' within non-poor households. The household unit of analysis acts to conceal such inequalities in distribution, for example between men and women or between different generations. Cantillon argues that the existence of differing living standards within households has serious implications for policies aimed at eliminating poverty.

Atkinson *et al.* (2002) note that if the interest is in disaggregating poverty data and considering the position of population sub-groups, then there may be a case for extending the dimensionality of equivalence scales to take account of characteristics apart from the household size and composition. For example, in the case of disability, research on expenditure by families with disabled children has shown how estimates can be made of the additional costs.

Despite these shortcomings, equivalence scales do provide a means to make adjustments for factors which have important welfare implications such as the size and composition of a household. Although many different scales exist, the OECD modified scale has gained widespread international acceptance (DWP, 2003). What is most important, however, is that the same equivalence scale is employed over time in order that longitudinal comparisons can be made.

Income distribution and measures of income inequality
The income distribution ranks households from lowest to highest in income terms, most often according to equivalised disposable income. Decile shares identify what proportion of total income is held by each population group so that the percentage share of total income of the bottom 10 per cent and up to the top 10 per cent can be analysed. Similarly, the distribution can be split into quartile or quintile shares for the purposes of such analysis. The usual way of arranging the information is in the form of a frequency histogram which shows the proportion of the population falling within each income band.

Trends in the degree of inequality in the income distribution can be identified by looking at the changes in the shares over time. This can be illustrated graphically using a Lorenz curve, which is constructed by plotting the proportion of the national income received by different percentages of the population when the latter are cumulated from the bottom. If there was full equality, such that the bottom 20 per cent received 20 per cent of the total national income, then the Lorenz curve would lie along the diagonal of the diagram – the line of complete equality. The further that the curve is from this diagonal, the further is the distribution from full equality and therefore the greater the inequality. The position of the Lorenz curve therefore provides a useful indication as to the extent of inequality in a given income distribution.

Furthermore, the Lorenz curve permits the comparison of the degree of inequality in two distributions. In Figure 2.1 the Lorenz curve for distribution A lies everywhere above that for distribution B. As such, distribution A can be regarded as unambiguously more equal than distribution B. In this way it is possible to use the Lorenz curve to make rankings of countries.

Figure 2.1: *Example of a Lorenz curve*

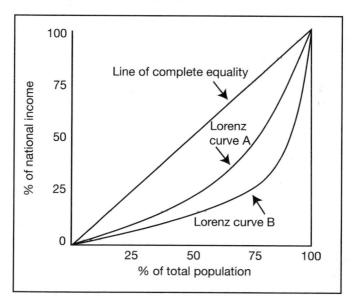

The Gini coefficient is a commonly used summary measure of inequality, which can take values from 0 to 100 per cent. It can be interpreted simply as the ratio of the area between the line of complete equality and the Lorenz curve to the total area of the triangle. It shows the relationship between cumulative shares of the population arranged according to the level of income and the cumulative share of total income received by them. In a situation of perfect equality, where every person receives an equal income, the Gini coefficient would be 0 per cent. A Gini coefficient of 100 per cent indicates total inequality and implies that the entire national income is held by one person.

Atkinson *et al.* (2002) note that, from the standpoint of inclusion, a key concern relates to the gap between the bottom and the top of the income distribution. The use of ratios allows us to examine this relationship. The quintile share ratio is the ratio of total equivalised income received by the 20 per cent of persons with the highest income (top quintile) to that received by the 20 per cent of persons with the lowest income (bottom quintile). Another ratio that is commonly used is the decile share ratio, which shows the ratio of the income share of the top 10 per cent to that of the bottom 10 per cent. In concentrating more on the extremes, this ratio places greater demands on the reliability of the data because the shares of decile groups are more subject to influence by outliers.

Cantillon (2000) advises care in the interpretation of summary measures because they tend to conceal distributional judgements. Citing the example of the Gini coefficient, she points out that such a figure tells us nothing about the welfare of different groups in the society being measured.

Relative income poverty measures
If we adopt a relative conceptualisation of poverty, we accept that poverty will be defined in relation to the living standards of a particular society at a particular date. In these circumstances, our concern is with individuals whose incomes fall below an acceptable minimum relative to the general level of incomes. The relative income standard is based solely on a criterion of low income, without regard to any independent condition or state of need. It is essentially a poverty line set relative to current income. A standard is defined in terms of income and those with incomes below that standard are classified as poor.

The rationale behind relative income poverty measures is that those falling below a certain proportion of what can be considered 'normal' income levels for a particular society are unlikely to be able to participate fully in the life of that society. This is the approach most commonly used to measure poverty in industrialised countries today. Fixed proportions of mean or median income (40 per cent, 50 per cent, 60 per cent or 70 per cent) are used. The Benchmarking and Indexation Group (2001) notes that a focus on the numbers below a particular line does not take account of the depth of poverty of these households. For this reason, studies, such as those undertaken by the ESRI, often use a number of these poverty thresholds to obtain a fuller view of the extent and depth of financial poverty.

The most commonly applied threshold had been 50 per cent of *mean* equivalised disposable income. In 1998, however, Eurostat proposed using 60 per cent of *median* income and this is now the most widely used threshold across Europe. It was selected to provide a degree of continuity with the 50 per cent of mean income measure. However, international organisations such as the UN and OECD favour a threshold of 50 per cent of median income.

At EU level, relative income measures form part of the suite of 'Laeken indicators' developed by the Indicators Sub-Group of the EU's Social Protection Committee and adopted by the European Council in Laeken in 2001. The Indicators Sub-Group recommended that the 60 per cent threshold relative income measure should be viewed as a measure of people who are 'at risk of being poor', in recognition of the fact that income on its own has limitations as an indicator. For this reason it has been labelled the 'low income rate'. Therefore, the share of persons with an equivalised income below a given percentage of the national median income is referred to as the 'at-risk-of-poverty rate', with anyone with an equivalised income of less than 60 per cent of the median, for example, considered to be 'at risk of poverty at a 60 per cent level' (CSO, 2005b).

Callan *et al.* (2004a) identify two central features of relative income poverty measures. First, they rely entirely on household income as the indicator of resources, living standards and capacity to participate in society. The income concept is weekly disposable income. Second, the benchmark of adequacy used in assessing whether a household has sufficient income moves strictly in line with the average (or median) income in the society.

Relative income poverty measures have a number of strengths. The UK's Department of Work and Pensions (2003) notes their ability to gauge the extent to which poor families' incomes are rising in relation to the economy generally, which in turn assists the process of targeting resources appropriately. Townsend (1997) observes that most European states conduct income and expenditure surveys which provide information about the income distribution of each country, facilitating analysis and standardised cross-national comparisons. Another advantage associated with such measures is that they involve less complex statistical calculations than others and are more easily understood. Furthermore, Hills (2004) argues that measures based on relative income provide robust information on trends over time.

There are also criticisms. For instance, Gordon and Pantazis (1997) argue that, while the relative concept of poverty is now widely accepted, there is still considerable debate about how to apply the concept to produce scientific measurements of poverty. Layte *et al.* (2004) suggest that the use of relative income poverty measures in isolation can produce misleading results as to the level and causes of poverty due to a range of shortcomings associated with such measures.

Townsend (1979) sees two limitations with this approach to the measurement of poverty. The first relates to the fact that income varies according to household size and formation. Although a distribution could be worked out for each household type, a point is reached beyond which it is not possible to allow for further differentiation among households. The second issue relates to the arbitrary nature of the choice of a particular percentage of the mean. Why choose 50 per cent of the mean (or median) as constituting relatively 'low' income over 60 per cent or any other percentage? The choice made, subject to the limitations imposed by considerations of data quality, has been shown to impact significantly on the derived estimates of the size and structure of the poor population.

Gordon *et al.* (2000b) cite the example of the UK, where, depending on whether 40 per cent, 50 per cent or 60 per cent of average income is used, poverty estimates of between 6 per cent and 32 per cent can be obtained. Additional factors impacting on these results include whether the self-employed are included and whether income is measured before or after housing costs.

Townsend (1997) argues that if poverty is a concept that is truly measurable, then the selection of a poverty line that distinguishes the 'poor' from the 'non-poor' is not an arbitrary matter. Yet Ringen (1988) concludes that there is no alternative for researchers except to choose a poverty line on their best judgement, argue in favour of it and hope that it is accepted as a reasonable approximation for poverty in that society at that time. If it is not accepted as such, then it is for the researcher to propose a revised poverty line.

Another limitation relates to the shortcomings in the income data on which relative income measures are based. As disposable income does not take account of a range of items including non-cash state benefits, occupational benefits-in-kind, housing costs and capital assets, it can be argued that median equivalised disposable income, as currently measured, may not adequately capture the concept of 'normal' or 'average' living standards which is fundamental to the measurement of relative poverty (Benchmarking and Indexation Group, 2001).

Another feature of the relative income poverty standard that has been criticised is that, as a measure, it masks the fact that the real incomes of the poor may also have risen. As Atkinson *et al.* (2002) explain, poverty measured by such relative standards will remain more or less stable, even if there is a constant and marked improvement in living standards, as long as the distribution of income remains the same. Thus, when the population as a whole shares improvements in prosperity, the numbers that could be said to be living in relative income poverty could, in theory, stay the same even though they are noticeably better off.

The converse also applies. In the case of economic decline, for example during a recessionary period, a general decline in living standards of the population affecting everyone equally may leave unchanged, or even reduce, the number of people experiencing relative income poverty. In this scenario, relative income measures would conceal the fact that the incomes of people relying on welfare payments may actually have declined in real terms. Ringen (1988) captures this phenomenon succinctly when he says: 'With the use of this criterion, measured poverty will change only, if and when, the distribution of income changes. Measured poverty will be the same in two societies with the same distribution of income even if the level of income is twice as high in one than in the other. No poverty will be recorded in a society where all are equally poor'. This leads him to conclude that relative income measures are little more than abstract statistical exercises which give little consideration to how people actually live.

Even though a range of low-income thresholds can be used and adjustments made for differences in household size and composition, Gordon *et al.* (2000b) question how meaningful these thresholds really are. The fact that a household is above or below a particular threshold says nothing about whether it has sufficient income for its members to live decently. Townsend (1997) maintains that selecting such cut-off points low on the income scale is not related to any strict criteria of need or deprivation. Relative income measures, therefore, do not tackle the issue of 'income adequacy'. Rather, it would be more meaningful to produce statistics which show the number of households which do not have an adequate income to allow them to participate in the economic, social, cultural and political life of their country, while at the same time avoiding poverty.

The Benchmarking and Indexation Group (2001) points to a number of other problems with the use of relative income indicators in isolation. First, by focusing on current income only, no account is taken of the way resources have been accumulated or eroded over time – factors which play a key role in influencing the likelihood of current deprivation and exclusion. Second, measuring those below a particular income threshold at a given point in time tells us nothing about the persistence or mobility of such households at that income level – a key factor in determining their relative living standards.

Mean or median income
Median income is distinct from a simple arithmetical average, or mean, in that it is solely concerned with identifying the position of the individual

household which is located at the fiftieth percentile (that is, the exact halfway point) of the overall equivalised distribution. It is concerned only with the rank ordering or distribution of households. Mean or average income, on the other hand, is obtained by dividing the total income of the population by the number of people in it.

Atkinson (1998) contends that the choice as to whether to use median or mean income is in part a matter of their relative statistical properties. For example, it can be argued that the median is less subject to sampling fluctuations. As such, the median is preferred because the mean or average income in a sample may be quite sensitive to a small number of very high incomes reported at the top of the distribution. This can affect the way relative income poverty lines based on the mean fluctuate over time. The median, however, is not affected by outliers in the same way.

The NESC (2005b) develops this point by providing examples of certain changes in household income which would affect the mean income of an income distribution but which would not cause the median to change. At the top end of the distribution, if a senior executive, whose household income is already significantly over the median, receives a bonus, this will not alter the position of the person at the middle of the distribution. Therefore, the median remains the same. The mean, however, would rise because overall income in the population, as a result of the bonus, has risen. At the bottom end of the distribution, if households on very low incomes receive an increase in welfare allowances, but such increases are not sufficient to bring them up to the median, then the position of the median is not altered. However, again, average income would rise because the increases to these households will raise the overall income in the population.

An important theoretical implication associated with the use of the median is that poverty can be eliminated. If, building on the example above, everyone on incomes below 60 per cent of median income received a boost to their incomes such that they all had incomes just above the 60 per cent threshold, poverty would fall to zero. This is because the position of the median is not altered by changes below it. Using the mean, however, it is not possible to eliminate poverty in this way because by increasing the incomes of those below a percentage of average income, overall income increases with the result that average income and the poverty threshold rise.

The NESC (2005b) points to a further implication relating to the clustering of households around the median-based poverty threshold. Depending on the extent of such clustering, a policy which affects households at this income level could lead to significant increases or decreases in the relative poverty rate, while bringing about very little change in the overall level of the income distribution.

Townsend (1979) argues in favour of using the mean over the median. He suggests that mean income provides a more 'stable' reference point for measuring the dispersion of incomes between countries and between two periods of time. This is because it is derived from the distribution of aggregate income. Where the interest lies in making cross-country comparisons, use of the median could potentially conceal a country's 'income capacity' if a tiny percentage of the population have exceptionally high incomes. In such cases, the proportion of the population of such a country with income less than 50 per cent of the median might be the same as another country, yet the proportion with less than 50 per cent of the mean could be twice as large.

Atkinson *et al.* (2002) observe that changing from the mean to the median can have different implications for different countries. This is because the ratio of the mean to the median can vary across countries.

Anchored or real income measures

Atkinson *et al.* (2002) point out that there are two measurement options in terms of observing relative poverty trends over time. As noted above, the poverty line could be uprated by the overall increase in living standards (average income). An alternative is to define the poverty line as a fixed proportion of mean or median equivalised income at a certain 'base date' and hold it constant in purchasing power terms. This would mean that it would be uprated in line with consumer price inflation only. This latter approach is often referred to as the 'anchored poverty line'. Anchored relative measures of poverty are sometimes referred to as 'absolute poverty' measures because they show the numbers below a fixed line that is not related to contemporary incomes or living standards. However, this measure should not be confused with the notion of 'absolute poverty' employed by international organisations such as the UN and which relates to those below minimum subsistence levels. Anchored relative measures are important in terms of gauging whether the poorest families are seeing their incomes rise in real terms. Atkinson *et al.* suggest that with sufficient economic growth, poverty measured in this way could be expected to fall quite rapidly.

Atkinson (1998) distinguishes between a constant real income standard and an absolute standard. The difficulty with using measures based on real incomes is that perceptions of poverty change as living standards rise. Would Rowntree's primary poverty line of 1899, uprated in line with consumer prices, really tell us much about modern-day poverty? For this reason, Atkinson concludes that such measures must contain provisions for periodic revisions. However, this raises the question of how often such revisions should take place – for what length of time should a constant real standard be applied? After a period of significant change, the price-adjusted line may no longer be regarded as acceptable. Its credibility risks being undermined.

The fact that relative income measures are rooted in the income distribution has led some to conclude that the share of the population living on incomes below 60 per cent of median income should be understood more as a measure of income inequality than a measure of poverty. For the NESC (2005b), relative income measures are widely used internationally not only because they provide trends of income inequality but also because they provide a measure of 'a degree of income inequality judged sufficiently serious as to impact negatively on people's social and economic opportunities, social standing, well-being and health'.

Expenditure

Budget standards

When a particular standard of living is defined, the budget standards method is used to price a specific basket of goods and services which is considered by experts to represent the standard of living in question. This approach to the study and measurement of poverty is used by a number of countries, including the US, Germany and Italy, to determine official poverty lines. The method, while accepting income as the correct measure, argues that expenditure may represent a better indicator of 'true' income. Budget standards look at expenditure on a basket of goods as a means of determining what an adequate level of income should be. The budget required to purchase the basket of goods is adopted as an income standard. This approach to the study and measurement of poverty predominated in the late nineteenth and early twentieth centuries.

Looking at the issue of adequacy, the Family Budget Unit at the University of York distinguishes between two budget standards. The first is termed a 'low cost but acceptable' (LCA) standard. This is the standard of living which, if achieved, enables people to avoid poverty, taking into consideration psychological, social and physical needs. It allows for warmth and shelter, a healthy and palatable diet, social integration and avoidance of chronic stress. The second budget standard, known as the 'modest but adequate' (MBA) standard, is more 'generous', focusing on what is required to obtain a lifestyle that is above the poverty level but well below the level of luxury. This 'reasonable' standard is, therefore, not only concerned with the avoidance of poverty but also with ensuring social inclusion. It allows for an individual having a healthy lifestyle and playing a full part in society.

For Atkinson *et al.* (2002), the main advantage of budget standards is that they are very 'tangible'. Townsend (1997) argues that the practical and specific nature of budget standards make them both publicly and politically plausible. The European Commission suggests that expenditure tends to be a more reliable proxy for 'true' income than the income reported in budget surveys (Atkinson, 1998). This may assist in addressing the problem of under-reporting of income in household surveys.

One of the main drawbacks of budget standards, however, relates to the choice of goods and services that make up the basket. This selection is reliant on the normative judgement of 'experts' in terms of what they see as constituting minimum needs. The views of such experts may or may not reflect the views of people generally. The role of experts therefore introduces an element of arbitrariness into this method. As Atkinson (1974) notes, the issue of where precisely the poverty line is drawn ends up depending on the judgement of the researcher, with the result that the notion of a purely 'physiological' basis to the poverty standard is lost. Atkinson *et al.* (2002) argue that the fact that judgements are involved means that the minimum budgets obtained will be more likely to be influenced by the standards and lifestyles prevailing in that particular country at that particular time. The budget standard must, therefore, be updated and adapted to reflect rising levels of prosperity and changing patterns of consumption. This raises issues about the cross-national and cross-temporal comparability of such standards.

Another drawback relates to the considerable time and costs involved in its implementation. This is due to the need to assemble a team of experts to decide on the contents of the budget, the process of obtaining the necessary pricing data for the basket of goods and services in respect of different types of households in different circumstances and the need to update the standard periodically so that it remains relevant.

Townsend (1997) concludes that the examination of household expenditure does not provide an answer in terms of what level of income is required by different households. This answer can only be obtained, in Townsend's view, by looking across society's groupings of individuals, households and communities at activities, customs, patterns and role obligations to determine whether there is a high correlation between the level of activity, deprivation and the level of income. Piachaud (1987) reaches a similar conclusion, stating that, on its own, a budget standard is not sufficient to determine 'any comprehensive poverty level'.

The food-ratio approach

The calculation of the poverty line using the food-ratio approach involves estimating the average share of household income spent on the defined basic needs and calculating the income levels at which different types of households spend a certain percentage in excess of the average on such necessities. It makes the assumption that households which spend the same proportion of their incomes on certain basic items such as food, clothing and heating are equally well off (Atkinson *et al.*, 2002). The poor are, therefore, distinguished from the non-poor by the proportion of their income spent on these basic items.

In 1964, the United States introduced an official poverty line based on a hybrid budget standards methodology. The US Department of Agriculture compiled estimates of the costs of food required by families of different composition. As in the case of Rowntree's studies, food requirements are derived from research into nutritional adequacy. With this information 'economy food plans' were developed (Gordon *et al.*, 2000b). The poverty threshold for a family is calculated by multiplying the cost of the relevant economy food plan by different amounts depending on the family size. These multiples are intended to reflect the proportion of average total income spent on food. The assumption is made that as income falls, all expenditure on food and non-food items is reduced proportionately until food expenditure equals the cost of the economy food plan. At this point food expenditure is considered to be at a minimal but acceptable level. The poverty line was adjusted over time only on the basis of the Consumer Price Index (Atkinson *et al.*, 2002). In this way the US poverty line has similar features to the 'anchored' relative income poverty threshold outlined above.

The American poverty line has been described as 'crude' by modern standards (Gordon and Pantazis, 1997). In 1995, the Panel on Poverty and Family Assistance, established to review the way the official poverty line is measured, issued recommendations for a revised approach which proposes that the median annual expenditure on the necessities of life be calculated for a reference household consisting of two adults and two children. A percentage of this expenditure is added in respect of expenditure required for other non-essential items to yield the poverty line for this household type. The poverty lines for other household types are calculated by applying equivalence scales to the reference household (Atkinson *et al.*, 2002).

As with budget standards, the food-ratio approach does not lend itself to international comparisons given that the differences in poverty rates may be due to different spending patterns rather than differences in deprivation levels.

The statutory method/state's standard

The statutory poverty line, or state's standard, corresponds to the income supports provided by a country's social welfare system. As such it amounts to the 'political translation of an established view on poverty' (Atkinson *et al.*, 2002). Townsend's seminal research in the late 1970s found that the statutory method reflected the views of a large section of the population (see Townsend, 1979). Household and individual income and expenditure data derived from surveys is compared with entitlements for statutory income support to produce estimates of the number of people with incomes below, at or above this level or in poverty by the standard accepted by society itself. It is important to distinguish between a measure of the number of households depending on social welfare and the number of households experiencing financial poverty. This is because social welfare rates may be above the poverty line, meaning that recipients are not 'poor'.

Atkinson *et al.* (2002) question whether social welfare rates accord with genuinely felt social need. Rates tend to be set in accordance with budgetary considerations and criteria and consequently are not guaranteed to keep recipients out of poverty. Also, the utility of statutory poverty lines is limited because they serve as both a goal and a tool of social policy. This ambiguity gives rise to a paradox whereby a generous government, which raises social welfare rates, in effect raises the poverty line; whereas a more frugal government, which allows rates to fall in real terms, reduces the poverty line (Hills, 2004). Finally, Atkinson *et al.* (2002) note that social welfare schemes do not exist in all countries and among those countries where schemes are in operation, their nature and scope differs significantly. For these reasons, the statutory method of poverty measurement does not lend itself to cross-national comparisons.

The subjective approach

It is possible to derive an income poverty line based on the subjective views expressed by the population itself. Piachaud (1987) terms this a 'social consensus' approach. It involves calculating a poverty standard based on the results obtained from survey responses to questions about the adequacy of income. For example, households might be asked what they consider to be the lowest net monthly income they require 'to make ends meet', in order 'not to be poor' etc. All methods of estimating a subjective poverty threshold make use of such a 'minimum income question' (MIQ). Gordon *et al.* (2000a) propose that the simplest and most democratic way of producing a subjective income poverty line is to use the average response to the MIQ for the population as a whole.

For Piachaud (1987) and Gordon (2000), a key virtue of this method is that it rules out the need for self-appointed 'experts'. It allows for the identification of the 'poor' according to standards that have been laid down by society. This results in more socially realistic income thresholds. However, expert involvement is inevitable in terms of setting questions and interpreting answers and this can give rise to some elements of arbitrariness.

Piachaud (1987) points out two conceptual issues associated with the subjective approach to the measurement of poverty. First, respondents' answers are liable to be influenced by their notions of the purposes of the study. Second, the view expressed by the majority may not accord with the experience and views of those on low incomes.

Atkinson *et al.* (2002) draw attention to other difficulties with subjective income methods. First, small changes in how the MIQ is worded can have a significant impact on the results obtained. This may be one of the reasons why subjective measures have been found to fluctuate over time within a given country. Second, in common with a number of the other approaches to poverty measurement outlined, there are difficulties in making cross-national comparisons because they will reflect differences in public perceptions and social conditions. Atkinson (1998) observes that when public opinion is involved in determining minimum income requirements, the result is a poverty line that tends to rise in real terms. Such poverty lines also tend to be higher than absolute or relative income poverty lines (Gordon, 2000; Atkinson *et al.*, 2002; Gordon *et al.*, 2000a).

Piachaud (1987) concludes that, as a means of defining poverty, such subjective approaches are of little help. For Ringen (1988), such measures are not valid because they involve accepting that people are poor because they feel they are poor. Poverty is not about feelings but rather about experiences in terms of how people live.

2. Deprivation/non-monetary measures of poverty

It is now common to think of poverty in terms of exclusion from a society's normal way of life due to a lack of resources. It is universally accepted that poverty is about more than just low income, being concerned also with the standard of living that people have. As noted earlier, definitions of poverty have been framed in these terms since the 1970s and influenced the definition set out in Ireland's 1997 National Anti-Poverty Strategy.

These definitions view poverty in terms of deprivation, implying that those who are measured as poor should be experiencing various forms of what is judged by a society to be deprivation. For Ringen (1988), this is a legitimate way to view poverty in developed 'European-type' welfare states, where the subsistence view of poverty is no longer relevant. Yet it has been common to measure poverty defined in such terms using relative income measures. Ringen argues that such an approach is not viable because what is defined is not measured and what is measured is not defined. This point is echoed by Atkinson *et al.* (2002) and Layte *et al.* (2004), who note the importance of income in determining a household's living standards but stress its limitations, particularly when used in isolation, as a measure of poverty and social exclusion. This is because a range of resources available to a household, of which cash income is only one, determine the wellbeing of that household (Nolan, 2002). Other resources include accumulated consumer durables at the disposal of the household, past savings, and goods and services provided by the state in terms of healthcare, education and housing.

Approaches to measuring deprivation
In the 1970s, Townsend (1979) sought to develop a methodology that would put the measurement of poverty onto a 'scientific footing'. By surveying 2,000 households across Britain, he aimed to derive a poverty threshold based on the interaction between household income and deprivation scores on an index constructed from a set of non-monetary indicators. By taking account of resources other than income a measure of 'relative deprivation' could be obtained, which Townsend argues is the only logical approach available to distinguish poverty from inequality.

Townsend selected twelve items which were used to identify a threshold point in the income distribution that could be regarded as indicating poverty. The deprivation index was intended to encompass the main aspects of dietary, household, familial and social deprivation but no one item could be regarded of itself to be a symptom of deprivation. Townsend's theory was that in descending the income distribution there would be a series of different points for different household types where deprivation increased disproportionately to the fall in income. Participation would also decrease disproportionately because people would increasingly be unable to engage fully in the 'style of living' considered normal for a given society. He tentatively concluded that such a threshold may exist and identified the poverty line/threshold at 150 per cent of the supplementary benefit standard. Piachaud (1987), however, is of the view that the existence of a threshold at which a clear shift in behaviour occurs is unproven.

Townsend's pioneering approach has been criticised for the role of choice and different tastes in the construction of the index. For example, McKay and Collard (2004) argue that merely choosing to do without certain items cannot be regarded as poverty. Gordon *et al.* (2000b) observe that a 'good deprivation measure' must distinguish between choice and constraint if cost-efficient poverty and social exclusion policies are to be developed and monitored. Another criticism relates to the use of the index itself. It is argued that aggregating all of the deprivation indicators into a single index favours a one-dimensional view of poverty over the more generally accepted multi-dimensional view (Cantillon, 2000). Finally, the use of a list of items defined by the researcher leaves the process exposed to an element of subjectivity and arbitrariness in terms of what items should be on the list and how many items someone has to lack to be considered poor. Townsend (1974) concedes this point, accepting that adopting this approach would not lead to the elimination of 'values'. He does, however, argue that such values will at least have been 'pushed one or two stages further back' with the result that the measurement process becomes less subjective and more dependent on 'externally assessed criteria'.

A second approach involves the production of a 'consensual' measure of deprivation, also known as 'perceived deprivation' (Townsend, 1997) and the 'deprivation indicator' approach (Gordon, 2000). The consensual approach to poverty holds that there is homogeneity across the population over what are regarded as the necessities of life. This method was developed by Mack and Lansley in the UK in 1985, building on Townsend's earlier work. They set out to answer the question 'How poor is too poor?' and to identify the minimum acceptable standard of living for Britain in the 1980s by seeking to define poverty in terms of an enforced lack of socially perceived necessities. This, they hold, contrasts with Townsend's earlier work which defined poverty in terms of exclusion from the 'norm', 'customary' or 'ordinary' living patterns.

Mack and Lansley made a number of methodological refinements in response to some of the criticisms levelled against Townsend's work. They set out to ask people directly what consumption items everyone should be able to afford, thus eliminating the value judgements of the researcher in favour of a consensual judgement of society at large about people's needs. In doing so, they consider that they have moved towards what Sen (1982) has termed 'an objective diagnosis of conditions' based around 'an objective understanding of feelings'. Halleröd et al. (1997) identify three advantages to taking a consensual approach. First, it represents poverty as a social phenomenon; second, there is a greater chance of securing public support for the definition; and third, poverty research based on a more widely accepted definition stands a greater chance of influencing and shaping political decisions and social policy.

In a second refinement, Mack and Lansley sought to measure poverty on the basis of enforced deprivation scores so that, instead of looking only at items people did not possess, they focused on a distinction between lacking items through choice and lacking items through an inability to afford them. Those who reported that they lacked three or more of the items regarded as necessities by a majority of the population ('socially perceived necessities') were regarded as poor. This stems from their finding that a strong correlation existed between low income and the enforced lack of three or more deprivation indicators. This became known as the consensual poverty line.

For Halleröd *et al.* (1997) and Gordon (2000), Mack and Lansley's consensual definition of poverty is one of the most important contributions to modern poverty research. It has formed the basis of a number of subsequent studies in the UK, for example the Poverty and Social Exclusion (PSE) survey carried out in 1998/1999. This survey added further items to the list of necessities, mainly focused around children and social activities, thus broadening the emphasis to encompass social deprivation as well as material deprivation. The survey found considerable 'social consensus' about necessary items (Gordon *et al.*, 2000a). Similar approaches to measuring the standard of living have since been adopted in a range of other countries including Ireland, Sweden, Denmark, Finland, the Netherlands, Belgium, Germany and Vietnam.

However, Hills (2004) points out that there are grounds for criticism in that Mack and Lansley's approach still involves 'expert' judgements in terms of the items included in the list which people are surveyed on. Although respondents decided which items on the list were necessary, it was Mack and Lansley who selected the forty-four items that appeared on the list in the first place.

Also, an element of arbitrariness remains in terms of the number of items which someone has to lack before being considered poor. Why choose three over two or four? If it is asserted that all of the items are necessities, could it not be argued that a person is deprived if they lack even one of them? The decision to regard as a necessity any item that more than 50 per cent of the population considers necessary is also an arbitrary one. Why not choose 60 per cent or 70 per cent?

Piachaud (1987) alludes to another issue thrown up by Mack and Lansley's work concerning the fact that many of those who were found to lack necessities did not lack 'non-necessities'. Cigarettes, for example, were classified as a non-necessity by respondents, yet 42 per cent of respondents reported buying a packet of cigarettes every other day. For Piachaud, this raises the issue of whether a household that cannot afford necessities but can afford non-necessities is really poor.

Ringen (1988) proposed another way of measuring the concept of relative deprivation based on the following assumptions: 'exclusion from one's society and community' can best be viewed in terms of a state of generalised deprivation; and such generalised deprivation is brought about by a combination of low income and a low level of consumption. This second condition implies that those experiencing poverty in the sense of relative deprivation will be a subset of those identified as being on a low level of income. Such poverty rates will be, by definition, lower than rates based on estimates of low income alone. This combined approach has been operationalised in Ireland in the form of the consistent poverty measure (see below).

Deprivation indicators

Deprivation is generally measured by asking people in a survey whether they have a particular item or participate in a particular activity. In asking such questions it is essential to distinguish between 'doing without something' and 'being deprived of something' (Collins, 2004). As we have noted, the first involves choice based on tastes and preferences, whereas the second is enforced, indicating the presence of deprivation. Atkinson *et al.* (2002) note that the concept of enforced deprivation in effect combines the monetary and non-monetary dimensions of poverty and social exclusion. These questions produce indicators of deprivation which focus on exclusivity from normal living patterns.

McKay and Collard (2004) usefully summarise the steps commonly taken today to measure deprivation in a robust way. These include:

1. Survey to gauge which of a number of items people consider are necessities and which should be affordable to everyone.
2. Establish which of these items respondents have, which items they lack because they do not want them and which items they lack because they cannot afford them.
3. Add up the number of items that people cannot afford from the list of those that a majority deem essential.
4. Derive the threshold where a shift in the level of deprivation occurs.

Atkinson *et al.* (2002) argue that deprivation indicators can provide a more direct measure of exclusion at a given point in time than relative income measures. This is because one of the difficulties with relative income measures is that some of those on low incomes will not be experiencing high levels of deprivation or exclusion. Using deprivation indicators, therefore, allows us to identify those specifically experiencing generalised deprivation and exclusion and to gain an insight into the underlying trends of an individual's or a household's wellbeing.

Deprivation indicators are an effective way of tracking changes in poverty over time. They can illuminate trends in changing standards and expectations about what society considers to be necessities in a way that is easily conveyed and understood. Townsend (1997) asserts that the popular perception of what constitutes the necessities of life and what is affordable provides 'an independent criterion' for the construction of a poverty line; and the UK's Department of Work and Pensions (2003) suggests that deprivation measures 'resonate well with the public perception of poverty'.

Gordon (2000) argues, with reference to the findings of the PSE survey carried out in the UK in 1998/1999, that, even though many respondents have difficulties with subjective poverty questions, the results obtained are as reliable and valid as other scientific methods. Also, the results tend to be available more quickly and at significantly lower overall costs.

One of the main drawbacks associated with the use of deprivation indicators was touched on earlier and relates to the fact that experts, as Piachaud (1987) observes, 'are not so easily disposed of'. In seeking to define a minimum acceptable standard of living for a society, someone inevitably has to set the questions to be asked and to interpret the results received. Another significant drawback is that, at present, there is no generally accepted approach to the use of deprivation indicators in the measurement of an agreed concept of relative poverty across different countries (Atkinson *et al.*, 2002).

3. Combined income–deprivation measures: Ireland's consistent poverty measure

It was Ringen (1988) who proposed that poverty could be measured by the double criterion of income and deprivation in consumption. He found that measuring poverty according to the incidence of low income tended to produce higher but more stable results. Measuring poverty by combining deprivation indicators with relative income measures tended to produce lower rates which were found to decline over time. The distinction stems from the observation that not all those on low incomes experience deprivation. Examining the results of the 1999 PSE survey in the UK, Gordon *et al.* (2000a) found that over 40 per cent of the poorest one-fifth of the population in income terms did not suffer from multiple deprivation and consequently could not be considered poor according to the double criterion of income and deprivation.

Ireland was one of the first countries to pioneer a combined approach to poverty measurement. The consistent poverty measure was developed by the ESRI using the findings of the 1987 Survey of Poverty, Income Distribution and Use of State Services (Whelan *et al.*, 2003). This approach involves looking at the numbers falling below relative income thresholds and also reporting the enforced lack of a common set of basic necessities to obtain a measure of what is termed the 'consistently poor'. It assesses the extent to which those on low incomes may be excluded and marginalised from participating in activities that are considered the norm in that society. Nolan (2002) explains that the core finding which underpinned the development of this measure was that the cross-sectional relationship between income and deprivation is weaker than many assume. Those experiencing deprivation are likely to be below the poverty line but may also be above it. The ESRI's analysis demonstrates that, while current income does play a role in determining the level of deprivation, other indicators of longer-term resources and needs are also important.

The ESRI sought to select a list of basic necessities which would best serve, together with income, as indicators of generalised deprivation. Factor analysis revealed a cluster of items that 'every household should be able to have and that nobody should have to do without' (Nolan, 2002). As Layte et al. (2000) explain, these items, possessed by most people, reflect rather basic aspects of current material deprivation and cluster together.

The eight items taken to indicate generalised deprivation due to a lack of resources are falling into debt to pay everyday household expenses and not being able to afford: heating, a substantial meal once a day, new rather than second-hand clothes, a meal with meat, chicken or fish every second day, a warm overcoat, two pairs of strong shoes or a 'roast' or equivalent once a week. A series of secondary indicators were also identified as part of this process, for example a car or a telephone. A third dimension contained household and related durables which, while they provided valuable information about current living standards, were not satisfactory as indicators of generalised deprivation.

People are defined as being in consistent poverty if they have an income below the relative income poverty threshold (i.e. with an equivalised disposable income that is less than 60 per cent of the median) and are living in a household deprived of one or more of the eight basic deprivation items.

Therefore, the consistently poor are, as Ringen (1988) postulated, a subset of all those that fall below the 60 per cent of median income line. Combining indicators of deprivation with income lines produces a very different perspective on trends in poverty than using income poverty lines alone. The ESRI found that, when benchmarking against other features commonly associated with generalised exclusion such as low levels of savings and high levels of economic strain and psychological distress, the consistent poverty measure performed much better than measures based on income alone (Layte et al., 2000).

For Hills (2004), there are a number of advantages associated with combined income–deprivation measures. First, they help to produce a more 'robust separation' between the poor and the non-poor in society by helping to identify a group that is clearly poorer than the rest of the population at a given point in time. Research shows that those who are both 'income deprived' and 'materially deprived' are distinctly different from the 'non-deprived' (DWP, 2003). Second, they serve as a useful complement to relative income measures, providing a valuable alternative perspective, particularly at times when living standards are changing rapidly. Third, they are attractive from a political point of view as if it can be shown that a person is poor on both counts (i.e. has a low income and is experiencing deprivation) it is hard to argue that they are 'undeserving' of assistance.

Combining the low-income threshold with deprivation indicators helps to overcome one of the difficulties associated with material deprivation measures alluded to above, namely, choice. With the addition of low income, the risk is greatly reduced that a respondent who states that they cannot afford certain basic necessities is not poor but is instead opting to spend their income on items not included in the list of basic necessities.

Combined measures such as the consistent poverty measure help to provide a more rounded and comprehensive view of the extent and experience of poverty than is possible when relying on relative income measures alone. Nolan (2002) points out that households identified as consistently poor are considerably more likely to report serious difficulty in making ends meet and psychological distress, and also to have significantly lower levels of savings. This, he argues, lends credence to the notion that the combined income–deprivation approach is more effective than income alone in identifying those truly 'excluded' due to their lack of resources.

Hills (2004) outlines some drawbacks with combined measures. They tend to rely on statistical techniques which are not transparent. Also, difficulties can arise when making longitudinal comparisons because if the items which make up the deprivation index side of the measure do not change over time, the combined measure, in effect, becomes an absolute standard. Equally, comparisons over time become problematic if the index is modified on a regular basis. Layte *et al.* (2000) point out that, in a scenario where those on low incomes share in the benefits of growth and experience a significant improvement in their living standards, a key concern is that a poverty measure incorporating a deprivation index fails to capture a deterioration in their relative situation.

Although the consistent poverty measure is unique to Ireland, approaches using income together with other information to identify the poor have also been developed in other countries. In the UK, Gordon *et al.* (2000a) produced a similar measure by carrying out statistical analysis on the results of the 1999 PSE survey. They found that the enforced lack of two necessities when combined with low income best discriminated between being poor and not poor. What was distinct about the approach taken in this study was that the deprivation items were 'popularly defined', being identified as basic necessities by a majority of the population. Also in the UK, a study by the Department of Work and Pensions in 2003 advocated a new approach to the measurement of child poverty which includes a combined income–deprivation measure.

Although the subject of ongoing consideration at EU level, a combined measure is not currently included in the Laeken suite of social inclusion indicators. Atkinson *et al.* (2002) explain that, applied in a European context, such a measure would effectively represent a combination of a common (European) deprivation standard, using a generally accepted set of basic necessities across all member states, and a country-specific relative income standard, reflecting income levels in each member state. An alternative would be for each member state to use a country-specific set of deprivation items representing what was generally regarded as constituting deprivation in that country together with the relative income standard. Atkinson *et al.* suggest that there would be significant challenges associated with achieving consensus on a methodology to identify an appropriate set of items for each country and how these should be updated over time and also with communicating to the European public what such a measure means and the rationale for the selection of the items included in it. Yet these are prerequisites if a combined income–deprivation measure is to be adopted as a key EU social indicator. This leads them to conclude that, for the time being at least, non-monetary deprivation indicators and combined income–deprivation measures incorporating such indicators, are likely to best serve country-specific efforts to gauge the level of poverty.

3

Poverty in Ireland

The Irish policy context

The consideration of poverty and issues relating to the measurement of poverty in Ireland today is a function of the policy framework which has evolved domestically and at European level by virtue of Ireland's membership of the EU.

Domestic policy

A number of significant developments helped to shape the domestic policy sphere in relation to poverty issues. These include the establishment of the Combat Poverty Agency, the work of the National Economic and Social Council, the advent of social partnership and the formulation of Ireland's first National Anti-Poverty Strategy.

The Combat Poverty Agency (CPA), established in 1986, has worked as a catalyst for change, seeking, through its activities and the research it has commissioned, to influence public policy and to elicit public support for action on poverty issues.

The National Economic and Social Council (NESC) was established in 1973 with the task of analysing and reporting on strategic issues relating to the efficient development of the economy and the achievement of social justice. For many years, the NESC was one of only a few bodies undertaking strategic, long-term analysis of Ireland's position and problems. In 2005, it published a key report entitled *The Developmental Welfare State,* which sets out a vision for the Irish welfare state that is intended to shape Ireland's approach to social policy issues for the next number of years (NESC, 2005a). For this reason, it is a key element of the policy framework within which the issue of poverty measurement must be considered.

The NESC played a key role in the development of a social consensus during the economic crisis of the mid-1980s, laying the foundations for the social partnership process which has been in place for more than twenty years. Social partnership has made an important contribution to the evolution and development of policies aimed at combating poverty and social exclusion in Ireland. As O'Donnell and Thomas (1998) point out, the second social partnership agreement, the Programme for Economic and Social Progress, which ran from 1990 to 1993, initiated an innovative approach to long-term unemployment. This involved the establishment of 'partnership companies', on a pilot basis, in twelve areas of acute socio-economic disadvantage. The objective of these structures was to promote a more coordinated, multi-dimensional approach to social exclusion.

In 1993, the National Economic and Social Forum (NESF) was established as a new partnership body, broadening the partnership process beyond the 'traditional social partners' (government, employers, trade unions and farming interests) to include representatives from organisations in the community and voluntary sector and members of the Oireachtas.

The negotiations on the Partnership 2000 agreement, which covered the period from 1997 to 2000, made the social partnership process even more inclusive by incorporating a 'third strand' – the 'social pillar' – comprising such organisations as the Irish National Organisation of the Unemployed (INOU), the Community Workers Co-operative and the Conference of Religious of Ireland (CORI). The result was an action programme aimed at achieving greater social inclusion through the National Anti-Poverty Strategy, tax and social welfare reforms to enhance work incentives, measures to address educational disadvantage and measures aimed at consolidating the local partnership approach to economic and social development.

Issues of poverty and social exclusion are comprehensively dealt with in the current social partnership agreement, Towards 2016. This agreement includes a number of important innovations. First, it has adopted the lifecycle framework set out by the NESC in *The Developmental Welfare State*. The lifecycle approach is intended to reorient the way policy is developed and public services are delivered around the needs of people at different stages of their lives. The main lifecycle stages are children, people of working age, older people and people with disabilities. Second, the agreement is for a much longer timeframe – ten years, reflecting the need to put in place long-term strategies to deal with complex social problems.

Launched in 1997, the National Anti-Poverty Strategy (NAPS) was formulated as a response to the UN World Summit for Social Development in Copenhagen in 1995, where Ireland along with 116 other countries agreed to a programme of action aimed at achieving a substantial reduction in overall poverty and inequalities. The NAPS placed poverty reduction firmly within government policy and set a series of medium-term targets. It also provided for the 'poverty-proofing' of relevant government policies, which involves evaluating their impact on poverty.

The NAPS provided a framework for actions to help achieve the objective of eliminating poverty in Ireland. It adopted a global poverty-reducing target framed around the consistent poverty measure developed by the ESRI. The target was to reduce the numbers living in consistent poverty from 9 to 15 per cent of the population to less than 5 to 10 per cent of the population. In addition, goals for the ten-year period from 1997 to 2007 were set under five key themes: unemployment, educational disadvantage, income adequacy, urban disadvantage and rural poverty.

The NAPS was reviewed in 2001 in accordance with commitments given in the Programme for Prosperity and Fairness that it would be updated, in consultation with the social partners, in order to ensure it remained current and relevant following five years of rapid economic growth. The underlying methodology and existing targets were reviewed and revised. New targets were also considered in the areas of child poverty, women's poverty, health, older people and housing/accommodation. The government's response to the consultative review is set out in *Building an Inclusive Society*, which was published in 2002. The revised strategy contains some thirty-six poverty reduction targets across a range of policy areas. These targets relate to all those groups considered vulnerable to poverty and social exclusion.

In February 2007, the National Action Plan for Social Inclusion 2007–2016 (NAPinclusion) was launched. The plan consists of a range of priority goals and actions for tackling poverty and social exclusion framed around the lifecycle approach. Significantly, it adopts a new poverty reduction goal: 'to reduce the number of those experiencing consistent poverty to between 2% and 4% by 2012, with the aim of eliminating consistent poverty by 2016, under the revised definition'.

Developments at EU level

The Lisbon European Council in 2000 agreed a strategic goal of making the EU 'the most competitive and dynamic knowledge-based economy in the world, capable of sustainable economic growth with more and better jobs and greater social cohesion' by 2010. A key component of this strategy is to make a decisive impact on the eradication of poverty and social exclusion by 2010.

For Atkinson (2003), two key steps have contributed to the recent development of the 'Social Europe'. These are the establishment of national action plans as part of the open method of coordination, and the agreement by member states on a set of European social indicators to be used to assess progress towards social goals, which include the eradication of poverty.

Inspired in part by the pioneering approach taken by Ireland in terms of its 1997 National Anti-Poverty Strategy, the EU Commission asked each member state to prepare a National Action Plan against Poverty and Social Exclusion (NAPsincl) to support the achievement of the 2010 goal. The aim was to translate the EU-level objectives into the national policies of each member state, taking into account individual national circumstances and social policy priorities. Objectives and a common outline for the national action plans were agreed in 2000.

Ireland's first NAPsincl covered the period from 2001 to 2003; a second plan covered 2003 to 2005. In 2006, new streamlined arrangements were put in place at EU level involving the production of a single report covering the areas of social inclusion, pensions and health/long-term care. The National Report on Strategies for Social Protection and Social Inclusion was submitted by Ireland in September 2006 and covers the period to 2008.

In December 2000, EU member states agreed a set of common objectives for combating poverty and social exclusion. In order to facilitate measurement and comparison of the outcomes of member states' policies to achieve these objectives, a set of eighteen common indicators, known as the 'Laeken indicators', was agreed in December 2001. These indicators, developed by the Social Protection Committee and its Indicators Sub-Group, were organised in a two-tier structure: primary indicators and secondary indicators (see Appendix 1) covering four dimensions of social inclusion: financial poverty, employment, health and education. The ten primary indicators are intended to cover the fields considered to be the most important elements contributing to social exclusion. The eight secondary indicators describe other aspects of the problem and are intended to support the primary indicators. There is also provision for a third tier consisting of indicators that member states themselves decide to include and which should complement the EU's common set of indicators.

In keeping with the spirit of the open method of coordination, member states agreed common objectives and the indicators by which performance is to be judged across the EU but were free to select and design the policies intended to achieve these objectives (European Commission, 2004). This approach also reflects the concept of subsidiarity which applies to Euro-pean social policy and which means that policy to combat poverty and social exclusion is first and foremost the responsibility of the member state.

Thus, common indicators do not imply common policies. While common indicators are needed to monitor progress in combating poverty and social exclusion in a comparable way, given the different models of welfare state across the EU, they must be regarded as performance indicators only, complementing the range of policy indicators employed at national level.

While all member states make use of the Laeken indicators in their national action plans, they do so in various ways and to different extents. Some countries set explicit targets, others do not. Most countries complement the commonly agreed indicators to a greater or lesser extent with a number of country-specific or 'national' indicators, for example the consistent poverty measure in Ireland.

The Indicators Sub-Group has continued to refine and develop the original list of Laeken indicators. For example, in July 2003, it was agreed to provide a focus on the situation of children by including a standard breakdown by age of all the Laeken indicators; to redefine the population living in jobless households indicator; and to include a new indicator of in-work poverty.

Key data sources

Statistics on the experience of poverty in Ireland, based on the measures outlined in Chapter 2, are derived from a number of sources including the ESRI's Living in Ireland Survey, the EU Survey on Income and Living Conditions which superseded it, and a range of other surveys carried out by the Central Statistics Office such as the Census of Population and the Household Budget Survey.

With the exception of the Census of Population, a common concern associated with all of these surveys is how representative the samples surveyed are of the overall population. For this reason, Nolan *et al.* (2000) caution that the results obtained must be seen as estimates which are subject to error.

Living in Ireland Survey
The Living in Ireland Survey (LIIS) ran from 1994 to 2001 and involved the collection of data by the ESRI through national household surveys. It included the Irish component of the European Community Household Panel (ECHP) survey, an EU-wide harmonised longitudinal survey reporting on the income and labour situation in member states.

The same households were surveyed in successive years to elicit information on their social situation, financial status and general living standards using a standardised questionnaire. The panel was selected so as to form a representative sample of the households and individuals in each country and the questionnaire was compiled using a series of internationally agreed questions determined by Eurostat, supplemented by a number of questions of national interest. The household questionnaire was completed by the household reference person who is responsible for the accommodation, and each individual in the household aged sixteen or over also completed an individual questionnaire. The main topics covered in both questionnaires are set out in Appendix 2.

Layte *et al.* (2001b) point out that the panel nature of the survey is particularly useful in highlighting the dynamics and persistence of poverty. That is, it reveals the extent to which people are trapped on low income for a number of years or move in or out of poverty from one year to the next. The surveys have been a valuable source of data for the NAPS and provided the basis for a series of ESRI reports on poverty and social exclusion in Ireland. Another advantage of these surveys was that they provided for inter-country comparisons.

There were a number of shortcomings associated with the survey and Corrigan *et al.* (2002) allude to the limited sample size, which meant that analysis of particular local areas or smaller social groups was not always possible, and the fact that the panel format embodied an element of attrition over time as a number of respondents dropped out. Whelan *et al.* (2003) point out, however, that the high attrition rate had a relatively minor impact on the sample distribution of individual and household characteristics. The LIIS also tended to involve a time lag of twelve to fifteen months between data collection and publication of figures because of the labour-intensive and time-consuming nature of tasks such as entering, cleaning and preparing the data for analysis.

EU Survey on Income and Living Conditions
In 2003, the ECHP was replaced at EU level by the EU Survey on Income and Living Conditions (EU-SILC). The EU-SILC is conducted by the Central Statistics Office (CSO) and, like the ECHP, is an annual survey intended to obtain information on the income and living conditions of different types of household. An important function of the EU-SILC is to collect information on poverty and social exclusion, incorporating the Laeken indicators and reflecting the importance that the European Council and Commission attach to combating these issues. At national level, the EU-SILC underpins the NAPS framework by providing data to monitor and evaluate progress towards achieving the targets set out in the strategy.

As a panel survey, the ECHP was susceptible to sample attrition and panel effects. To overcome these problems, data for the EU-SILC is required in both cross-sectional (pertaining to a given time in a certain time period) and longitudinal (pertaining to individual-level changes over time) dimensions. This means that only some households are surveyed on an annual basis. Also, information is collected continuously throughout the year, with up to 130 households surveyed each week to give a total sample of 5,000 to 6,000 households in each year. The income reference period for the EU-SILC is a floating one, that is, it is the twelve months prior to date of interview rather than the standard calendar year for the LIIS/ECHP. The EU-SILC's larger sample size and cross-sectional survey design also mean that it is more effective for analysis of small sub-groups of the population and its results are more directly comparable with those from national sources.

Results from the first survey, relating to the year 2003, were published in January 2005 (CSO, 2005a). However, the 2003 results were later revised by the CSO to take account of improved re-weighting and calibration methods in line with EU recommendations, these were published alongside the 2004 results in late 2005 (CSO, 2005b).

Census of Population

The Census of Population is a valuable source of data for poverty research chiefly because, by attempting to capture all persons in the state, it allows for analysis of small geographic areas and groups of people within society. Data can be broken down according to electoral divisions, of which Ireland has 3,400.

The 2002 Census included a range of new questions which yielded valuable data for use in the analysis of poverty, disadvantage and quality of life. These questions related to membership of the Travelling Community, commuting time, the provision of unpaid help or care, nationality, disability, computer ownership, third level qualifications and labour force participation. Census 2006 also included new questions on such issues as relationships, ethnicity and voluntary activity.

Drawbacks of the Census, as pointed out by Corrigan *et al.* (2002), include the considerable delay in the publication of results arising from the onerous task of processing returns, and the absence of an income question. A pilot survey for Census 2002 found that the inclusion of such a question had a significant adverse effect on response rates. International evidence supports this finding. However, without an income question it is not possible to calculate income-based poverty rates from Census data.

Household Budget Survey

The Household Budget Survey (HBS) has been carried out in Ireland since 1951. The eighth survey related to 2004/2005, the data from which had not been released when this analysis was prepared.

The main purpose of the HBS is to determine the current pattern of household expenditure in order to update the expenditure weights in the Consumer Price Index. A survey is carried out using a representative sample of all private households in the state. Respondents are required to keep a detailed account of household expenditure over a two-week period.

Although primarily an expenditure survey, the HBS also collects detailed income data and for this reason facilitates analysis of the income distribution. As well as earnings income, the survey collects information on welfare income, household tenure and possession of a medical card.

Key statistics and trends

Trends in relative income poverty

Table 3.1 shows how Ireland's unprecedented economic growth affected the evolution of median equivalised household disposable income (hereafter referred to as median income) between 1994 and 2004. In 1994, weekly median income stood at €128.10. Over the period to 2004, it increased by 141 per cent to €309.19. Given that the Consumer Price Index rose by approximately 35 per cent over the same period (CSO, 2005d), this points to very large real increases in median income. Significant growth in median income has implications for poverty lines derived from it.

Table 3.1: *Median income, 1994–2004**

	1994	1997	1998	2000	2001	2003	2004
Annual (€)	6,684	8,907	10,071	12,487	14,287	15,286	16,133
Weekly** (€)	128.10	170.70	193.00	239.30	273.80	292.96	309.19
Index of median earnings	100	133.3	150.7	186.8	213.7	228.7	241.4

* Using the national equivalence scale (1.00/0.66/0.33)
** Weekly median income is derived by dividing annual income by 52.18 (EU-SILC)
Sources: CSO (2005b) and own calculations

Relative income poverty rates measure poverty in terms of the percentage falling below income thresholds derived as fixed proportions of mean or median income. A threshold of 60 per cent of median income was proposed by Eurostat in 1998 and is now widely used throughout Europe. For this reason, the median is used as the basis for analysis in this section. In addition to the 60 per cent threshold, various other thresholds are used for comparison purposes.

Table 3.2 shows that the 60 per cent of median income threshold increased from €76.86 in 1994 to €185.51 in 2004. Therefore, significantly more income had to be earned in 2004 than in 1994 for a person to stay above the poverty line.

Table 3.2: *Weekly median income thresholds, 1994–2004**

	1994 (€)	1997 (€)	1998 (€)	2000 (€)	2001 (€)	2003 (€)	2004 (€)
50% of median income	64.05	85.35	96.50	119.65	136.90	146.47	154.59
60% of median income	76.86	102.42	115.80	143.58	164.28	175.77	185.51
70% of median income	89.67	119.52	135.09	167.53	191.66	205.06	216.43

* Using the national equivalence scale (1.00/0.66/0.33). Figures are calculated on the basis of the weekly median income figures in Table 3.1

Table 3.3 shows that the large increases in median income resulted in increasing numbers of people falling under relative income poverty thresholds over the period. Focusing on the 60 per cent of median income threshold, most of this increase occurred between 1994 and 1998, with the percentage peaking in 2001. The 50 per cent threshold paints a starker picture with the proportion falling below this threshold more than doubling by 2001 before falling back slightly by 2004. In contrast, however, the proportion of people falling below the 70 per cent of median income threshold was more stable over the period.

The fact that the proportions falling below the 50 per cent and 60 per cent of median thresholds rose faster than the proportion falling below the 70 per cent threshold suggests that for much of the period increasing numbers on very low incomes were falling further behind the median and slipping deeper into poverty.

Table 3.3: *Persons below median income thresholds, 1994–2004**

	1994 (%)	1997 (%)	1998 (%)	2000 (%)	2001 (%)	2003 (%)	2004 (%)
50% of median income	6.0	8.6	9.9	12.0	12.9	11.6	11.1
60% of median income	15.6	18.2	19.8	20.9	21.9	19.7	19.4
70% of median income	26.7	29.0	26.9	28.1	29.3	27.7	28.7

* Using the national equivalence scale (1.00/0.66/0.33)
Sources: Whelan *et al.* (2003) and CSO (2005b)

One of the key strengths of the relative income poverty measure is that it permits standardised cross-national comparisons. This is because it is based on income data which is widely available and which has been collected in a harmonised way across the EU member states. Eurostat produces figures for all member states based on data from the ECHP or EU-SILC surveys. Using this data it is possible to establish where Ireland ranks at European level in terms of relative income poverty. Figure 3.1 shows that in 2001 Ireland had the highest rate of relative income poverty, at 21 per cent, of all fifteen member states. The average for the EU-15 in that year was 16 per cent.

Figure 3.1: *Persons below 60 per cent of median income in the EU-15, 2001*

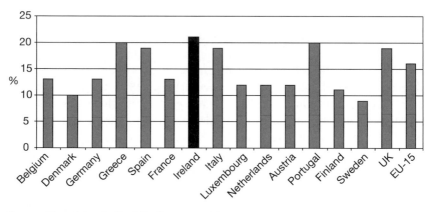

Source: Eurostat website: http://epp.eurostat.ec.europa.eu

The Eurostat figure of 21 per cent differs from the CSO figure of 21.9 per cent recorded for 2001 (see Table 3.3) because the EU uses a different definition of income to the one employed in Ireland. The difference centres on the treatment of pensions. Also, a different equivalence scale, the OECD modified scale, is used at European level.

Table 3.4 shows that Ireland's rate of relative income poverty has been consistently higher than the EU-15 average over the period from 1995 to 2004. Portugal, Spain, Greece, Italy and the UK recorded similarly high rates. In contrast, Sweden, Finland and Denmark enjoyed some of the lowest rates of relative income poverty over the period.

Another commonly used measure is relative income poverty 'anchored at a point in time'. This approach involves looking at the numbers falling below relative income thresholds over time, where those thresholds are held constant in real terms over the period, that is, they are uprated only in line with changes recorded in the Consumer Price Index each year. The 'anchored' approach provides a very different perspective on Irish poverty.

Table 3.4: *Persons below 60 per cent of median income in the EU-15, 1995–2004**

	1995 (%)	1996 (%)	1997 (%)	1998 (%)	1999 (%)	2000 (%)	2001 (%)	2002 (%)	2003 (%)	2004 (%)
Belgium	16	15	14	14	13	13	13	~	16	15
Denmark	10	~	10	~	10	~	10	~	12	11
Germany	15	14	12	11	11	10	13	15	15	16
Greece	22	21	21	21	21	20	20	~	21	20
Spain	19	18	20	18	19	18	19	19	19	20
France	15	15	15	15	15	16	13	12	12	14
Ireland	**19**	**19**	**19**	**19**	**19**	**20**	**21**	**~**	**20**	**21**
Italy	20	20	19	18	18	18	19	~	~	19
Luxembourg	12	11	11	12	13	12	12	~	10	11
Netherlands	11	12	10	10	11	11	12	11	12	~
Austria	13	14	13	13	12	12	12	~	13	13
Portugal	23	21	22	21	21	21	20	20	19	21
Finland	~	8	8	9	11	11	11	11	11	11
Sweden	~	~	8	~	8	~	9	11	~	11
UK	20	18	18	19	19	19	19	18	18	~
EU-15 average	17	16	16	15	15	15	16	~	~	~

* This table uses the OECD modified equivalence scale (1.0/0.5/0.3)

~ Data not available

Sources: Eurostat website: http://epp.eurostat.ec.europa.eu and CSO (2005b)

Whelan *et al.* (2003) used data from the LIIS for the period 1994 to 2001 and mean income as the basis for analysis (as opposed to median income which has since become the norm). Then, taking 1994 as the base year, mean or average income was increased over time only in line with the increase in prices. In stark contrast to the steadily rising trend in relative income poverty noted earlier, they found that the percentage of persons falling below a poverty line set at 50 per cent of mean or average income 'anchored' in 1994 fell quite significantly from 17.6 per cent in 1994 to 2.4 per cent in 2001. This measure reflects the scale of real income growth throughout the income distribution during this period. However, it must be borne in mind that such real income measures do not reflect the relative nature of poverty, which, as set out in the NAPS, is predicated on current norms and expectations.

People's life chances are also influenced by the length of time they spend in poverty. Layte *et al.* (2001a) observe that the longer a person spends below the relative income threshold, the more likely they are to remain in poverty. About 20 per cent manage to escape poverty after a year has elapsed; this drops to only 7 per cent after four years in poverty. Layte *et al.* also point out that if a person's experience in poverty is a short and temporary one, their life chances are unlikely to be seriously impaired. Long or persistent spells in poverty are more likely to be associated with the erosion of resources and higher levels of economic strain, psychological distress and fatalism.

Persistent poverty is included as one of the Laeken indicators and is defined as being below the 60 per cent of median income poverty line in the current year and for two of the three previous years. Due to the need to have data for a four-year period, the first figures for persistent poverty under the EU-SILC were not available when this analysis was conducted. However, using data from the LIIS, Whelan *et al.* (2003) calculated rates of persistent poverty for the period 1997 to 2001. In 1997, the rate of persistent poverty was 10.1 per cent, rising to 15.6 per cent by 2001. Although these rates are lower than the corresponding relative income poverty rates (18.2 per cent in 1997 and 21.9 per cent in 2001), Whelan *et al.* observe a worrying trend, namely that the persistent poverty rate in 1997 was 56 per cent of the relative income rate but by 2001 it had risen to 71 per cent of the relative income rate. Figure 3.2 illustrates these findings, which suggest that those in poverty in 2001 were more likely to be long-term poor (3+ years).

Who are the poor?
The data collected by the LIIS and EU-SILC surveys facilitate a more detailed analysis of the persons falling below relative income thresholds.

Figure 3.2: *Rates of persistent poverty and relative income poverty, 1997–2001*

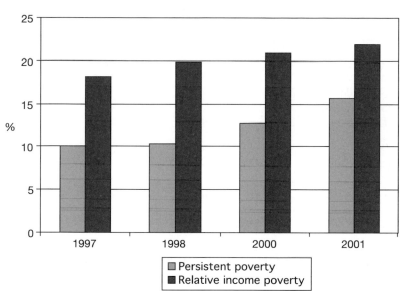

Source: Whelan *et al.* (2003)

The availability of data on the incidence of poverty broken down by variables such as household composition, age and labour force status helps policy-makers to pinpoint which groups in society are in greatest need of state assistance and in turn assists the process of targeting public resources.

It is useful to analyse the incidence of relative income poverty according to the composition of the household. Table 3.5 shows the percentage of persons falling below the 60 per cent of median income threshold for a range of different household types for the period from 1994 to 2004. As data from the EU-SILC is not broken down into as many categories as data from the earlier LIIS, the data relating to 2003 and 2004 is aggregated for the categories relating to two adults with one to three children, and for the categories relating to two adults with four or more children and three or more adults with children.

The most striking feature in Table 3.5 is the significant increase in the percentage of one-adult households falling below the 60 per cent line after 1994. The rates for households with two, three or more adults also increased over the eleven-year period but to a much smaller degree, while the proportion of lone-parent households (one adult and one or more children) falling below the poverty line remained high.

Table 3.5: *Persons below 60 per cent of median income by household type, 1994–2004*

	1994 (%)	1997 (%)	1998 (%)	2000 (%)	2001 (%)	2003 (%)	2004 (%)
1 adult	7.3	35.7	50.1	47.7	46.8	40.4	35.7
2 adults	6.8	9.4	16.2	23.1	28.8	21.2	21.4
3 or more adults	2.6	7.9	5.3	8.8	10.4	12.4	12.7
2 adults, 1 child	12.5	16.8	14.6	13.9	19.0 ⎫		
2 adults, 2 children	12.6	11.5	12.2	16.1	13.9 ⎬	12.3	12.5
2 adults, 3 children	21.8	20.4	20.6	20.7	20.8 ⎭		
2 adults, 4 or more children	44.0	38.9	29.8	39.2	40.7 ⎫		
3 or more adults with children	13.6	19.3	21.9	14.6	13.0 ⎭	23.2	23.1
1 adult with children	36.3	45.3	44.9	46.5	42.9	49.3	48.3
All	15.6	18.2	19.8	20.9	21.9	19.7	19.4

Sources: Whelan *et al.* (2003) and CSO (2005b)

Looking at the composition of persons below the 60 per cent median income line according to household composition, Whelan *et al.* (2003) point out that there has been a marked increase over the period in the importance of household types without children. In 2001, households comprising only adults accounted for 44 per cent of all those in poverty as against 11 per cent in 1994. This trend has continued in recent years, as shown in Table 3.6. By 2004, households comprising only adults accounted for just under half of all those in poverty. Lone parents accounted for a lower percentage (9.2 per cent) of all those below the poverty threshold in 2004 than in 1994 (10.2 per cent). This suggests a deterioration in the position of households with adults only relative to households with children. It may also point to the success of child income support payments such as child benefit, which has increased more than fourfold since 1997, in helping to lift families with children out of poverty.

Table 3.7 provides some insight into the risk of poverty for different age groups. The key observation from this data is the sustained and sizeable decrease in the relative incomes of the elderly compared to the population at large. Consequently, the risk of an individual over 65 years having at his/her disposal an equivalised income less than 60 per cent of the median rose from 5.9 per cent in 1994 to a high of 44.1 per cent in 2001 before falling back to 27.1 per cent in 2004.

Table 3.7 also indicates that child poverty, although higher than the overall relative income poverty rate each year, has fallen slightly over the period, which may provide further indication of the effectiveness, albeit

Table 3.6: *Persons below 60 per cent of median income by household composition, 1994 and 2004*

	1994 (%)	2004 (%)
1 adult	3.3	13.6
2 adults	5.5	19.4
3 or more adults	2.1	16.4
2 adults, 1 child	4.6 ⎫	
2 adults, 2 children	9.4 ⎬	15.9
2 adults, 3 children	16.4 ⎭	
2 adults, 4 or more children	26.8 ⎫	25.5
3 or more adults with children	21.8 ⎭	
1 adult with children	10.2	9.2

Sources: 1994 data from Whelan *et al.* (2003); 2004 data provided by the CSO on request

Table 3.7: *Persons below 60 per cent of median income by age, 1994–2004*

	1994 (%)	1997 (%)	1998 (%)	2000 (%)	2001 (%)	2003* (%)	2004* (%)
Children (under 18)	24.5	23.5	22.6	23.7	23.4	21.0	21.2
18–64	12.1	14.7	15.9	16.4	17.1	17.6	17.6
65+	5.9	24.2	32.9	38.4	44.1	29.8	27.1

* The EU-SILC employs a different age breakdown as follows: 0–14, 15–64 and 65+
Sources: Whelan *et al.* (2003) and CSO (2005b)

modest, of the successive increases in the rates of child benefit in helping to combat child poverty.

Labour force status provides a further insight into who the poor are in Irish society. Unfortunately, due to the use of a different set of classifications in the EU-SILC, analysis is restricted to the period covered by the LIIS (1994–2001). Table 3.8 compares the percentages of people below the 60 per cent of median income poverty line for each labour force category in 1994 and 2001. With the exception of two categories – the self-employed and the unemployed – a greater percentage of all categories was below the poverty line in 2001 than in 1994. Over half of the unemployed (51.4 per cent) were in poverty in 1994 and although the percentage had declined by 2001, 44.7 per cent were still classed as poor. The risk of poverty remained lowest for employees.

In sharp contrast, the position of those classified as ill/disabled, retired and on home duties suffered a marked deterioration during the 1990s. The percentages of the ill/disabled and those on home duties falling below the

Table 3.8: *Persons below 60 per cent of median income, and the composition of all those below 60 per cent of median income, by labour force status, 1994 and 2001*

	1994		2001	
	% of persons in each category below 60% line	*% of all those below 60% line*	*% of persons in each category below 60% line*	*% of all those below 60% line*
Employee	3.2	8.3	8.1	18.8
Self-employed	16.0	10.1	14.3	6.6
Farmer	18.6	10.6	23.0	7.6
Unemployed	51.4	41.1	44.7	7.3
Ill/disabled	29.5	6.2	66.5	11.9
Retired	8.2	6.0	36.9	18.8
Home duties	20.9	17.8	46.9	29.0
All	15.6	100.0	21.9	100.0

Source: Whelan *et al.* (2003*)*

60 per cent median income poverty line more than doubled from 1994 to 2001. The largest increase, however, was reserved for the retired. Figure 3.3 illustrates the changes between 1994 and 2001.

Figure 3.3: *Persons below 60 per cent of median income by labour force status, 1994 and 2001*

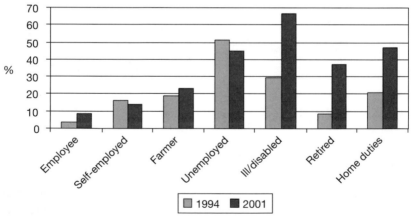

Source: Layte *et al.* (2004)

Table 3.8 also highlights the changing composition of the poor between 1994 and 2001. It clearly shows the significant improvement in employment prospects in Ireland over the period. In 1994, the unemployed made up 41.1 per cent of all those in poverty but by 2001 this figure had fallen to just 7.3 per cent. Although employment opportunities made a big impact on reducing unemployment over the period, Table 3.8 raises a question about the quality of the jobs being created. The fact that employees accounted for 18.8 per cent of the poor in 2001 compared to just 8.3 per cent in 1994 provides evidence of the emergence of a 'working poor'.

Again, we see the deteriorating position and increased vulnerability of groups such as the ill/disabled, the retired and those on home duties. These three groups together made up 30 per cent of the poor in 1994 but by 2001 this had doubled to 59.7 per cent of all those in poverty. Figure 3.4 illustrates the changed composition of poverty in Ireland between 1994 to 2001.

It can be concluded from the data in Table 3.8 that those dependent on social welfare (the ill/disabled, pensioners, the unemployed and those on home duties) face the highest risks of poverty in Irish society.

Figure 3.4: *Composition of persons below 60 per cent of median income by labour force status, 1994 and 2001*

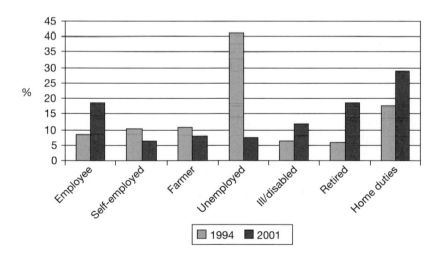

Source: Layte *et al.* (2004)

Consistent poverty trends
The global poverty reduction targets contained in the 1997 NAPS and the new NAPinclusion 2007–2016 are framed around the consistent poverty measure, which identifies the proportion of the population both below relative income poverty thresholds and experiencing basic deprivation. A

person is said to be experiencing basic deprivation if they are deprived of one or more basic deprivation items. Those in consistent poverty are, therefore, a subset of the population falling below relative income thresholds. For this reason, it can be expected that consistent poverty rates will be equal or, more likely, lower than relative income poverty rates.

Table 3.9 shows the evolution in the rates of consistent poverty from 1994 to 2004 using three relative income thresholds. Focusing on the now conventionally used 60 per cent threshold, we see that consistent poverty dropped steadily from 8.3 per cent in 1994 to 4.1 per cent in 2001. However, this trend was reversed in 2003 when a significantly higher rate of 8.8 per cent was recorded. The reason for this sharp reversal relates to the replacement of the ECHP by the EU-SILC.

Table 3.9: *Persons in consistent poverty at 50 per cent, 60 per cent and 70 per cent of median income, 1994–2004*

	1994 (%)	1997 (%)	1998 (%)	2000 (%)	2001 (%)	2003 (%)	2004 (%)
50% of median income	3.5	5.2	3.6	2.7	2.9	5.3	3.9
60% of median income	8.3	7.8	6.0	4.3	4.1	8.8	6.8
70% of median income	14.5	10.7	7.7	5.4	4.9	11.1	9.6

Sources: Whelan *et al.* (2003) and CSO (2005b)

There were a number of important methodological differences in the structure and design of the ECHP and the EU-SILC which resulted in a major discontinuity in the measurement of deprivation and, consequently, consistent poverty. Due to this discontinuity, the CSO and the ESRI have advised that, in terms of consistent poverty trends 'no conclusions can . . . be drawn regarding the direction or scale of any real changes between 2001 and 2003' (CSO, 2005a). It cannot therefore be concluded that consistent poverty worsened between 2001 and 2003.

The reasons for the differences have been investigated and centre on two main methodological issues. The first relates to differences in the question format used in the two surveys. The CSO (2005a) points out that the EU-SILC employs a 'direct questioning approach' using computer-assisted personal interviewing, which has been found in other surveys to result in higher reported levels of deprivation.

The second issue relates to the fact that the ESRI-conducted ECHP surveys were panel surveys, with the same people interviewed annually over a number of years, whereas households were interviewed for the first time for the EU-SILC. The CSO (2005a) points out that households that have previously participated in the survey tend to have different response patterns to first-time interviewees. Re-interviewing the same households over a number of years can give rise to what are known as 'panel effects'. For example, households that have previously participated in the survey may be somewhat more reluctant than others to reveal that they do, in fact, now face or continue to face, an enforced lack of some basic items in question. Also, households that have previously participated in the survey may have a greater awareness of the type of information that the survey seeks to ascertain and this may influence how they respond on the second and subsequent occasions they are surveyed.

The EU-SILC results for 2004 reveal a number of striking statistics. For example, almost one-third of lone-parent families (31.1 per cent) are consistently poor as are almost one in ten single-person households (9.9 per cent). Also, 20.7 per cent of those living in rented or rent-free accommodation are consistently poor as are more than one in five of the ill/disabled (21.7 per cent).

4

The Paradox of High Economic Growth and High Poverty

Difficulty stated

One difficulty associated with the use of relative income poverty measures relates to the paradox of high rates of economic growth existing alongside high and increasing rates of poverty. This paradox has given rise to serious credibility problems for this measure in Ireland and elsewhere.

Difficulty explained and justified

To illustrate the paradox of rising poverty rates during a period of unprecedented economic growth and prosperity in an Irish context, it is useful to highlight the key indicators of Ireland's economic performance between 1995 and 2004.

According to CSO data, Ireland's gross domestic product (GDP) and gross national product (GNP) almost doubled in real terms (constant prices) between 1995 and 2004, from €74.5 billion to over €145 billion GDP and from €68 billion to €121 billion GNP. The rates of growth in both GDP and GNP over the period averaged at 7.7 per cent and 6.6 per cent respectively, which far exceeded the corresponding average GDP/GNP rate of 2.3 per cent growth in the EU-15. Ireland was transformed from a country which had a GDP per capita below the EU average (89 per cent of the EU-15 average) to the country with the second highest GDP per capita in the EU (128 per cent of the EU-15 average). The numbers in employment also rose significantly, from 1.28 million to 1.9 million, and the unemployment rate fell from 12.2 per cent to 4.4 per cent. Such indicators led the NESC (2005b) to conclude that it is undeniable that living standards, measured in income terms at least, for the vast majority of people in Ireland improved in the decade from 1995 to 2004.

Despite this benign environment, relative income poverty, as measured by a line drawn at 60 per cent of median income, remained stubbornly high, rising from 15.6 per cent in 1994, peaking at 21.9 per cent in 2001 and falling back modestly to 19.4 per cent in 2004. The resulting situation saw Ireland have the second highest GDP per capita in the EU at the same time as it had one of the highest rates of income poverty.

As relative income poverty will continue to be used to assess Ireland's position compared to other EU member states – the 60 per cent of median income indicator is the first of the Laeken suite of social indicators – it is important to understand this paradox. Relative income measures are also used by a range of other international organisations such as the UN, UNICEF and the OECD.

Addressing this difficulty

There is no easy way to address the problem associated with this paradox. An important first step, however, particularly from a policy-making perspective, is to understand the causal factors behind Ireland's high rates of relative income poverty. These factors include income trends, earnings trends, demographic and structural issues, labour market trends, tax and social welfare policies, levels of social expenditure in a comparative context and the impact of certain 'transitory' groups such as students. Each of these causal factors is explored below.

Income trends
The period of remarkable economic growth to which the data above bears testament is also reflected in income and earnings trends. Median equivalised disposable income rose from €128.10 in 1994 to €309.19 in 2004, an increase of more than 141 per cent. Prices, as measured by the Consumer Price Index, rose by around 35 per cent over the same period. This effectively means that median equivalised disposable income more than doubled in real terms over the eleven-year period. This income growth has led to the rapid convergence of Irish average income with that of its larger and traditionally more prosperous neighbours such as Germany and the UK.

The effect of this growth in income is that relative income poverty lines have also increased substantially in real terms. However, the unequal distribution of this increased income contributed to a situation where significant increases in average household income, shared by those on lower incomes, were accompanied by increasing relative income poverty rates.

When it comes to the unequal distribution of income (income inequality), Ireland is something of an outlier in European terms. Nolan and Smeeding (2004) analyse how people with incomes at different points in the Irish income distribution in real terms compare with people at the same point in the distribution in other rich countries. They converted the incomes of a number of 'rich' countries into real 2000 US dollars and then, recomputing low, median and high incomes in these countries as a fraction of the US median, created 'real incomes' (see Figure 4.1).

Figure 4.1: *Real income wellbeing of all persons in nine countries**

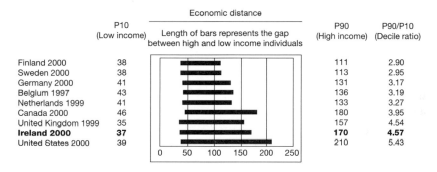

* As a percentage of overall US 2000 median equivalent income in PPP terms
Source: Nolan and Smeeding (2004)

Nolan and Smeeding find that those on low incomes in Ireland are worse off than those on low incomes in the other countries surveyed, with the exception of the UK. The position is particularly stark at the top end of the income distribution where the average 'rich' Irish person is 21 percentage points above the average of 149 per cent and 13 percentage points above the average 'rich' person in the UK. With a decile ratio of 4.57, the overall gap between low income (10th percentile) and high income (90th percentile) in Ireland was higher than in all the other countries except the US.

Looking at the composition of the Irish income distribution and how it changed during the 1990s provides an insight into how the increases in incomes were distributed amongst the population. Table 4.1, which is based on data from the LIIS, displays the decile shares in equivalised disposable income among individuals in 1994 and 2000. This data shows that the increases in equivalised disposable income during this period were distributed unequally. The growth in incomes between 1994 and 2000 had the effect of boosting the share of total incomes held by the middle and higher parts of the income distribution (4th to 9th deciles); in contrast, the share of total income held by the top decile and the bottom three deciles fell.

Median equivalised disposable income is by definition to be found at the mid-point of the income distribution – the point at which there are as many

Table 4.1: *Equivalised disposable income, 1994 and 2000**

Income decile	Share in total equivalised disposable income (%)	
	1994	*2000*
Bottom	3.8	3.2
2nd	4.9	4.5
3rd	5.6	5.5
4th	6.4	6.9
5th	7.5	8.0
6th	8.9	9.3
7th	10.6	10.8
8th	12.6	12.7
9th	15.3	15.6
Top	24.4	23.6

* Using the national equivalence scale (1.0/0.66/0.33)
Source: Nolan and Smeeding (2004)

people above as there are below. As we have seen, the significant increases in income benefited the middle of the income distribution disproportionately. These increases in turn led to the significant increases in median income and the relative income poverty lines derived from median income. The bottom deciles in 2000 were less well off relatively speaking than they were in 1994 when they had a larger share of total income. This suggests that the middle of the income distribution and higher deciles are pulling away from the bottom of the distribution and goes some way to accounting for the increasing numbers falling below the poverty line based on 60 per cent of median income.

Thus we can see that Ireland's significant economic growth was accompanied by rapid growth in income and, by extension, median income and the relative income poverty thresholds calculated as percentages of median income.

Earnings trends
Earnings from employment are the most important source of income in Ireland (NESC, 2005b). CSO data shows that gross average weekly industrial earnings increased significantly from €344.06 in 1994 to €560.77 in 2004. Earnings grew by 63 per cent in nominal terms and by 28 per cent in real terms given that prices rose by 35 per cent over the period.

Focusing on data from CSO surveys for the period 2000 to 2004, the NESC (2005b) observes a picture of considerable uniformity in gross earnings increases both sectorally and when broken down within sectors. However, analysing data from the ESRI's 1987, 1994 and 1997 household surveys, which cover the whole economy as opposed to specific sectors and allow for the overall distribution of earnings at individual level to be studied, Nolan (2001) finds that earnings at the top rose much more rapidly than at the middle and that lowest earnings kept pace with the middle. Although relating to an earlier period, it is possible that this trend continued from 1997 onwards.

The introduction of the minimum wage in 2000 was also influential. The establishment of a floor to (legal) earnings created an additional incentive to those on social welfare to take up employment and improved the living standards of those in the lowest paid jobs. As the minimum wage rises, more people are encouraged to take up entry-level jobs. Increases in the minimum wage help to safeguard the living standards of these employees. When the minimum wage was introduced in April 2000 it was set at €5.58 per hour and it has since been increased a number of times. The NESC (2005b) points out that the total increase of 37.1 per cent (to €7.65 from 1 May 2005) very closely mirrored the increase in gross average industrial earnings of 38.2 per cent over the same period. The minimum wage continues to rise and was set at €8.65 from 1 July 2007.

It is clear, therefore, that earnings growth and increases in the minimum wage are contributory factors to the growth in income and by extension the median income highlighted earlier.

Demographic and structural trends
The NESC (2005b) proposes that two notable changes in household composition in recent times have had an influence on the growth of median household income. First, the age structure of the Irish population shifted between 1991 and 2002 with the proportion of the population in the 25–64 age group, where labour market participation is most likely and earnings at a maximum, increasing from 44.8 per cent to 51.3 per cent. At the same time the proportion of the population aged under 25 dropped and the proportion over 65 remained relatively static. Therefore, median income was more likely than in the past to be driven by the income growth of people of working age.

Second, the patterns of Irish family and household formation evolved over the 1990s with the number of childless-couple and single-person (aged under 65) households increasing rapidly. These factors have combined to reduce the average equivalised household size. The effect of this change is that a given increase in household income could yield a greater rise in median equivalised household incomes.

Labour market trends
The most dramatic macroeconomic development in recent years has been the decline in unemployment and the marked increase in the numbers in

employment. Consequently, the number of 'jobless households' where no adult is in employment has decreased and the proportion of the population living in jobless households fell from 13.5 per cent in 1995 to 8.6 per cent in 2004 (CSO, 2005d).

The NESC (2005b) points out that the distribution of household incomes is affected not only by the distribution of an individual's earnings, but also by the degree to which those earnings are clustered into the same households containing more than one earner. Another feature of the recent transformation of the Irish labour market has been the increase in the number of dual income households, a trend driven by the increasing participation rates of women in the labour force. In 1995, 41.4 per cent of women of working age were in employment; by 2004, this figure had risen to 55.8 per cent (CSO, 2005d).

Russell *et al.* (2004) distinguish between 'work rich' households in which all adults are engaged in employment, 'work poor' households where no adult is in employment and 'mixed work' households where some but not all of the adults are engaged in the labour market. Table 4.2 illustrates the decline of the mixed work household, commonly characterised by the 'male breadwinner', and the rise of the work rich household where both spouses are in employment. Part of the increase in work rich households may also stem from the transition from unemployment to employment in single adult households (consisting of either single persons or lone parents).

Table 4.2: *Trends in household employment status, 1994–2000*

Adults aged 18 to 64	1994 (%)	1997 (%)	2000 (%)
No work (work poor)	22.1	17.6	13.6
Mixed work	42.9	46.1	37.1
All work (work rich)	34.9	36.4	49.3

Source: Russell *et al.* (2004)

Table 4.2 shows that the proportion of households where no adults are employed fell from 22.1 per cent in 1994 to 13.6 per cent in 2000. At the same time the proportion of households where all adults were working rose from just over one-third to almost one-half of all households. The fall in jobless households dependent on social welfare and the rise in work rich households are two factors that contributed to the sharp growth in Ireland's median equivalised disposable income and the associated poverty thresholds.

Callan *et al.* (2004a) illustrate this effect on poverty rates in a simulated analysis of the impact of labour market structure on relative income poverty rates. They standardised Ireland's labour market structure to that of the Netherlands, involving a reduction in the rate of unemployment and a shift in the composition of labour market participation from self-employment and unemployment towards employment. The simulation showed that benign labour market trends could, perversely, result in an increase in relative income poverty rates because the substantial rise in employment was accompanied by raised incomes, which in turn caused the relative income poverty lines to rise. Callan *et al.* found that there is the potential for more people to fall below the higher poverty line than will rise above it as a result of a general transition to employment.

Tax and social welfare policies

The labour market trends identified above have implications for tax and social welfare policy in terms of the beneficial impacts on the exchequer finances. Falling unemployment reduces welfare expenditure and rising employment boosts income tax revenue and social insurance contributions. This situation presents government with a range of tax and social welfare policy options, including increasing welfare rates and decreasing tax rates. Such policies influence the shape of the income distribution and have a significant impact on relative income poverty rates.

Social welfare policy

Economic progress allowed the Irish government to increase social assistance/insurance payments significantly. Between 1994 and 2004, unemployment assistance increased by 74 per cent, the contributory old age pension by 85.6 per cent and the one-parent family payment (including child benefit) by 79.6 per cent. Prices increased by around 35 per cent over the same period, which implies real increases of 39 per cent for unemployment assistance, 50.6 per cent for contributory pensions and 44.6 per cent for one-parent/one-child families.

These significant increases in real terms in the disposable income of individuals and households dependent on social welfare brought about tangible improvements in the standard of living of those on the lowest incomes. The key issue, however, is how these real increases compare to what was happening for everyone else in society. How do they compare to the increase in median equivalised disposable income, on which relative income poverty lines are based?

Median income grew by 141 per cent from 1994 to 2004. By extension the relative income poverty threshold, calculated as 60 per cent of median income, also grew by 141 per cent over the period. Discounting child benefit, which benefits all families with children regardless of their position on the income distribution, we see that the increases in social welfare rates, although significant in real terms, are well below the increases in median income and the relative income poverty line over the period. This means that those who were dependent on social welfare, relatively speaking, fared badly, which echoes the observation made earlier regarding the middle of the income distribution pulling away from the bottom.

A logical consequence of this phenomenon is that increasing numbers of social welfare dependents fall below the more rapidly rising 60 per cent median income poverty threshold. Data presented in Chapter 3 provides evidence of this: in 1994, 29.5 per cent of the ill or disabled, 8.2 per cent of the retired and 20.9 per cent of those on home duties (lone parents, carers etc.) were below the poverty line; in 2001, those figures had risen to 66.5 per cent, 36.9 per cent and 46.9 per cent respectively (see Table 3.8). Looking at the composition of all those below the poverty line we see that in 1994 the retired, the ill/disabled and those on home duties collectively accounted for 30 per cent of those in poverty. By 2001, this had risen to 59.7 per cent. The phenomenon of median income rising more rapidly than social transfers is widely acknowledged as one of the main reasons for Ireland's increasing rate of relative income poverty (Whelan *et al.*, 2003; Callan *et al.*, 2004a; Benchmarking and Indexation Group, 2001; Cantillon, 2000; Layte *et al.*, 2004; NESC, 2005b).

As a measure, relative income poverty masks the fact that those at the bottom of the income distribution, while faring less well relatively speaking, nonetheless gained considerably in real terms over the period under analysis. The tangible improvements for those on social welfare were matched and even exceeded by the improvements accruing to those higher up the income distribution, leaving those on social welfare worse off in relative terms. One of the key drawbacks of measures based on relative income therefore is the fact that any marked increase in living standards of those under the income line that is also shared by the rest of the population is not reflected in the numbers living in relative income poverty (Benchmarking and Indexation Group, 2001).

Taxation policy
One of the key drivers of the growth in Ireland's median income since the mid-1990s has been tax reform. Ireland's exceptional economic performance provided the government with the scope for significant cuts in direct taxation. Figure 4.2 illustrates how the taxation burden on the PAYE earner reduced from 1997 to 2004. It shows that the effective tax rate, that is the overall proportion of a person's income paid out in taxation, fell significantly. In the case of a single person on a modest income of €25,000, 33.7 per cent was deducted in 1997 and only 14.7 per cent in 2004.

Figure 4.2: *Effective taxation rates in Ireland, 1997–2004*

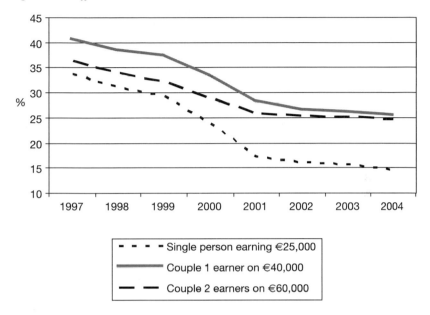

Source: Department of Finance (2003)

A number of measures were taken to reduce the burden of income tax over the period from 1995 to 2004. The standard rate of income tax was gradually reduced from 27 per cent to 20 per cent, and the higher rate from 48 per cent to 42 per cent, by 2001. The focus then shifted to widening the tax bands and increasing the threshold at which a person becomes liable for income tax. Such measures were aimed specifically at removing those on the minimum wage from the tax net.

At a time when there was considerable growth in gross average earnings, reductions in income tax served to boost net earnings further. While gross average industrial earnings grew by around 28 per cent in real terms between 1994 and 2004, net average industrial earnings grew by a much larger figure of 46 per cent in real terms over the same period (NESC, 2005b). As net earnings are a central component of household disposable income, tax reform has been another key factor behind the rapid rise in median income and the relative income poverty lines derived from it.

Another crucial issue relates to how equally the benefits of the tax cuts were distributed across the income distribution. Tax cuts focused on low-income earners might be expected to lead to a reduction in overall income inequality and in relative income poverty. By their nature, however, tax cuts are only going to be of benefit to those with a tax liability. Those whose incomes are too low to be liable for tax or who are dependent on social welfare will clearly not benefit from cuts in direct taxation.

This is the situation that predominated during the earlier part of the period under analysis, as is shown in Table 4.3. More recently, the ESRI has carried out an analysis on the overall distributive effect of successive budgets using the SWITCH (Simulating Welfare and Income Tax Change) tax-benefit simulation model. The ESRI takes the approach that the distributional impact of the budget is best measured relative to a 'distributionally neutral' benchmark or yardstick (Callan *et al.*, 2004b). This 'distributionally neutral' budget provides for equal growth in income across all income groups and thus provides for a more appropriate analysis of budgetary policy. Under such a budget, the main population groups would share equally in the benefits of economic growth with tax credits, tax bands and social welfare payment rates increased in line with expected growth in wage income. The actual outturn in each budget is then compared against this neutral benchmark to establish the redistributive impact.

Table 4.3 shows the combined effect on the income distribution of taxation and welfare policy in Ireland over the period of analysis. Between 1995 and 2001, the middle and upper quintiles of the income distribution emerged as the clear winners with the value of tax reductions outweighing the effects of social welfare rate increases at the bottom of the income distribution. The top 60 per cent of the distribution saw gains of between 11.8 per cent and 13.7 per cent compared with a decline in incomes of 1.9 per cent for the bottom 20 per cent.

From Budget 2002 onwards, however, a more progressive and redistributive approach reversed the earlier trends and benefited the bottom quintile in particular. Between 2002 and 2006, the bottom quintile saw gains of 17.4 per cent compared with only 0.4 per cent for the top quintile. Callan *et al.* (2004b and 2006) conclude that the overall impact, other things being equal, of Budgets 2005 and 2006 would be to reduce relative income poverty (based on 60 per cent of median income) by 0.5 per cent and 0.4 per cent respectively.

In summary, tax and social welfare policies since the mid-1990s have interacted to cause increasing numbers to fall below relative income poverty lines. The significant increases in social welfare rates were not sufficient to keep pace with the growth in the incomes of employment-rich households in the middle of the income distribution, who benefited, in the late 1990s in particular, from substantial reductions in income tax liability that boosted their net disposable income. The shift to a more progressive budgetary policy can be expected to have a beneficial impact on relative income poverty rates. Indeed some of the reduction in the poverty rates

Table 4.3: *Distributive impact of recent budgets*

Income quintile per adult equivalent	% change in income, actual policy over neutral benchmark	
	Budgets 1995–2001	Budgets 2002–2006
Bottom	–1.9	17.4
2nd	3.1	8.2
3rd	11.8	3.1
4th	13.7	1.6
Top	12.5	0.4
All	10.5	3.1

Source: Callan *et al.* (2006)

recorded for 2003 and 2004, as highlighted in Chapter 3, could be attributed to the more redistributive tax and welfare policies of recent years.

Social expenditure

Analysing the reasons for inter-country differences in relative income poverty rates, Callan *et al.* (2004a) find that social expenditure forms a lower proportion of national income in Ireland than it does in those EU countries with the lowest poverty rates. They conclude that there is a relationship between 'welfare effort' and relative income poverty rates, pointing out that an extra percentage point on social security expenditure as a proportion of GDP is associated on average with a reduction of 0.4 per cent in the relative income poverty rate.

Table 4.4 shows that Ireland's expenditure as a percentage of GDP and GNP in 2001 was among the lowest in Europe. Indeed Ireland's social protection expenditure as a percentage of both GDP and GNP was consistently below the EU-15 average over the period from 1994 to 2002. During the 1990s, social expenditure in Ireland fell as a percentage of both GDP and GNP. This, in part, was a symptom of the above-average GDP and GNP growth over the period, which outpaced real term rises in social expenditure. Since 2000, this falling trend has been reversed.

Callan *et al.* (2004a), Lawlor and McCarthy (2003) and others have set out reasons why one might expect Ireland's social protection expenditure to be lower than certain other European countries. These reasons include demographic factors related to the relatively low percentage of the Irish population of retirement age compared to other European countries where the 'ageing' of populations is already an issue; and the dramatic fall in unemployment in the late 1990s which was accompanied by reduced expenditure on unemployment benefit.

Table 4.4: *Social protection as a percentage of GDP, 2001*

	% of GDP spent on social protection		*% of GDP spent on social protection*
Sweden	31.4	Portugal	24.0
France	30.0	Poland	22.1
Germany	29.8	Luxembourg	21.3
Denmark	29.4	Iceland	20.2
Austria	28.6	Spain	20.1
Switzerland	28.2	Hungary	19.8
UK	27.6	Czech Republic	19.2
Belgium	27.5	Slovak Republic	19.1
Netherlands	27.5	**Ireland (% of GNP)**	**18.3**
EU-25	27.3	Malta	17.3
Greece	27.1	**Ireland**	**15.3**
Finland	25.7	Lithuania	15.2
Italy	25.6	Latvia	14.3
Norway	25.6	Estonia	14.3
Slovenia	25.5	Cyprus	N/A

Sources: CSO (2005c); percentage of GNP calculated using data from CSO (2005d)

However, Callan *et al.* (2004a) argue that, even when these factors are taken into account, Ireland's social expenditure is still low. Focusing on per capita rates of social assistance, they point out that social protection pensions to the elderly for example are clearly low relative to other European countries. Highlighting Denmark as a country with one of the lowest rates of relative income poverty in the EU, they compared the two countries' rates of social assistance as a percentage of average earnings for a number of groups in 1998 (see Table 4.5) and found that Irish payment rates were significantly less than their Danish equivalent in each case.

Using the EUROMOD tax-benefit model for Europe, Callan *et al.* (2004a) undertook a simulation to establish what the effect on relative income poverty rates would be if the Danish welfare system and level of payment rates were introduced in Ireland (together with adjustments to taxation to reflect the need for additional exchequer funding for such a system). They found that Irish welfare payment rates would have to be significantly increased. For example, weekly unemployment benefit would more than double from €89.52, as it was in 1998, to €194.13. The total gross cost of raising Irish social welfare payments to rates which formed the same proportion of average earnings as the Danish system would be in the region of €2.7 billion in 1998 terms. Both the standard and higher rates of income tax (as they were in 1998) would have to be increased from 24 per cent to 35 per cent and from 46 per cent to 57 per cent. The impact on

Table 4.5: *Payment rates in relation to average earnings for key social welfare schemes in Denmark and Ireland, 1998*

Single adult	Denmark (%)	Ireland (%)
Pensioner		
Maximum	34.7	27.7
Minimum	34.7	24.2
Unemployed		
Maximum	52.2	23.6
Minimum	42.8	22.9
Ill/disabled		
Maximum	54.9	24.1
Minimum	34.7	22.9
Social assistance	31.3	22.9
Social assistance (lone parent)	41.6	23.6

Source: Callan *et al.* (2004a)

relative income poverty (defined as 60 per cent of median income) would be to reduce it from 17.5 per cent to just under 13 per cent.

Callan *et al.* conclude that 'differences in social security policy could account for a substantial proportion of the difference in relative income poverty rates between Ireland and Denmark'. Their research demonstrates a link between social expenditure and relative income poverty and suggests that sizable increases in social welfare payment rates could lead to lower rates of relative income poverty. The fact that such social welfare rates have increased significantly in recent Irish budgets may go some way to explaining the falls in relative income poverty that have been observed in 2003 and 2004.

'Students' and poverty
Table 4.6 shows that over 23 per cent of students fell below the 60 per cent of median income poverty threshold in 2003 and 2004, accounting for almost 10 per cent of all those below the poverty line in 2004.

'Students' is a somewhat unique category of principal economic status. One reason why so many students are classed as being in poverty is because their earnings capability is severely curtailed during the period of their studies. It could be argued, however, that their time in poverty will be temporary, given that they should be in a position to secure employment on qualification that will provide sufficient income to take them above the poverty threshold.

Another difficulty is that the student categorisation in the EU-SILC includes all those in full-time education aged 16 or over. Thus one

Table 4.6: *Persons below 60 per cent of median income by principal economic status, 2003 and 2004*

| | 2003 | | 2004 | |
	% in each category below 60% line	*Composition of those below 60% line*	*% in each category below 60% line*	*Composition of those below 60% line*
At work	7.6	16.0	7.0	14.8
Unemployed	41.5	7.6	37.2	6.4
Student	23.1	8.6	23.6	9.8
Home duties	31.8	22.5	32.1	23.1
Retired	27.7	9.0	26.1	9.1
Ill/disabled	51.7	9.1	47.3	8.8
Children	21.5	25.4	21.9	25.3
Other	33.9	1.9	52.3	2.7
All	19.7	100	19.4	100

Source: CSO (2005b); composition data obtained from the CSO

component of those students reported to be in poverty will be 16 and 17 year olds in secondary education. In order to focus on those in full-time third or fourth level education, a breakdown was obtained of students in poverty in 2004 showing those under 18 years (who are most likely to be still attending school) and those over 18 years (who are most likely to be in higher education). The data shows that 45 per cent of those students in poverty in 2004 were aged 16 or 17 and 55 per cent were aged 18 and over. As shown in Table 4.6, 9.8 per cent of all those in poverty in 2004 were classed as students. We now know that 55 per cent of this 9.8 per cent were aged 18 or over and were most likely to be in third level education. This group equates to 5.4 per cent of all those in poverty.

It could be argued that those students aged over 18 in particular are a transitory component of those in relative income poverty. If this group, accounting for 5.4 per cent of all those below the poverty line, was to be excluded from the analysis, the overall poverty rate of 19.4 per cent in 2004 would fall by 1.05 per cent (5.4 per cent of 19.4) to 18.35 per cent.

Conclusions and implications

Between 1995 and 2004, Ireland's GDP per capita rose from 89 per cent of the EU-15 average to over 128 per cent. Poverty, measured as the proportion of the population with incomes less than 60 per cent of the median, also rose from an already high level of 15.6 per cent in 1994, peaking at 21.9 per cent in 2001, to 19.4 per cent in 2004. The implications of this paradox for the credibility of such relative income poverty measures are clear.

No single factor accounts for this phenomenon. Rather it is the result of the interplay of a range of causal factors including:

- Growth in earnings which outpaced inflation
- Growth in income which outpaced earnings growth, particularly at the middle and higher end of the income distribution
- Demographic and structural trends which resulted in a reduction in the average equivalised household size
- Labour market trends in terms of the rise in the number of dual income households
- Tax and social welfare policies that saw increases in social welfare rates, although substantial in real terms, failing to keep pace with income growth at the middle of the income distribution fuelled by tax reform in the late 1990s
- Levels of social expenditure which were lower than the EU average, even when demographic and other factors such as unemployment were taken into account.

The number and complexity of these factors indicates that there is no easy way to address this paradox. However, an important first step from the perspective of the policy-maker is to understand these factors and how they interact to produce the rates of poverty seen in Ireland in recent years. There is also a clear challenge in terms of communicating and explaining the reasons for the paradox of high poverty and high economic growth to the general public.

Given that relative income poverty measures will continue to be used by international organisations such as the UN and the OECD, and at EU level by Eurostat, there is a case for building on the approach taken in the UN's *Human Development Report 2005*, which included an explanatory box entitled 'The Two Tales of Irish Poverty'. Highlighting the circumstances of the paradox outlined here, the box explains that 'when economic conditions change rapidly, relative poverty trends do not always present a complete picture of the ways that economic change affects people's lives' (United Nations, 2005).

The preceding analysis suggests that the trend of rising relative income poverty rates in Ireland since the late 1990s could be reversed in the coming years when a number of moderating factors come into play. Such factors include the significant increases to social welfare rates introduced in Budgets 2005, 2006 and 2007 and the move away from tax reforms that primarily benefited the middle of the income distribution.

Another important finding relates to the proportion of those below the poverty line who are students. The analysis found that approximately 5.4 per cent of all those in poverty are full-time students in higher education. On qualification, these students should be in a position to secure employment that will take them above the poverty line. If they were excluded from the analysis on the basis that their time in poverty is temporary, the poverty rate would fall by 1.05 per cent.

5

Misleading Cross-Country Comparisons

Difficulty stated

Another difficulty undermining the acceptability of relative income poverty measures arises when economically less-developed countries perform better than richer countries in cross-country comparisons of poverty rates. This unlikely outcome has become a particular issue for comparative analyses of EU poverty rates made in a post-enlargement context.

Difficulty explained and justified

According to the literature, one of the main strengths of relative income measures is that they facilitate analysis and standardised cross-national comparisons. This is because they are based on income data which is widely available, albeit with notable time lags, and which, in a European context, is collected and compiled on a harmonised basis using a common survey, the EU-SILC. The availability of harmonised income data is one of the reasons why income-based measures feature so prominently in the Laeken suite of social indicators. However, such cross-national comparisons of relative income poverty in the EU have become problematic, particularly post-enlargement, creating misleading impressions of the relative wellbeing of one country versus another.

Figures showing that a lower percentage of people in Hungary are in poverty than in Ireland, for example, compound the credibility problems associated with relative income measures and prompt policy-makers to ask whether such inter-country comparisons are meaningful. Table 5.1 illustrates these difficulties. It shows that Ireland has one of the highest poverty rates in the EU, ranked just behind Slovakia and Greece. In contrast, the Czech Republic has the lowest poverty rate, which implies that living standards in the Czech Republic are significantly better than they are in Ireland.

Fahey (2005) points out that the gap in living standards between the richest and poorest EU member states has widened since the eastern

Table 5.1: *Ranked relative income poverty rates* for EU member states, 2003***

	Relative income poverty rate (%)		Relative income poverty rate (%)
Greece	21	Cyprus	15
Slovakia	21	Lithuania	15
Ireland	**20**	Malta**	15
Spain	19	Austria	13
Italy**	19	Denmark	12
Portugal	19	France	12
Estonia	18	Hungary	12
UK	18	Netherlands	12
Poland	17	Finland	11
Latvia	16	Sweden**	11
EU-25	15	Luxembourg	10
Belgium	15	Slovenia	10
Germany	15	Czech Republic	8

* Based on 60 per cent of median income threshold. Eurostat figures differ slightly from national figures because a different equivalence scale (1.00/0.5/0.3) and a different definition of income are used
** Figures relate to 2003, except for Malta (2000), Italy (2004) and Sweden (2002)
Sources: Eurostat website: http://epp.eurostat.ec.europa.eu and CSO (2005b)

enlargement of the EU in 2004. The new member states, by and large, have median incomes that are much lower than the EU-15 countries. Figure 5.1 shows that the median household income of richer EU countries such as Denmark and Germany is up to three or four times greater than that of poorer member states such as Latvia. It also indicates the considerable discrepancies in the level at which poverty thresholds are set across EU states. In the case of Estonia, for example, the threshold was 2018 PPS, whereas in the Netherlands it was 9164 PPS.[1]

The existence of such disparities has implications when comparing the incidence of poverty between EU member states. This is particularly true in the case of Ireland, which had the highest rate of relative income poverty, at 21 per cent, of all fifteen EU member states in 2001. Figure 5.2

---

[1] PPS stands for Purchasing Power Standard. It refers to the artificial common reference currency unit used in the EU to express the volume of economic aggregates for the purpose of spatial comparisons in such a way that price level differences between countries are eliminated. Economic volume aggregates in PPS are obtained by dividing their original value in national currency units by the respective PPP (conversion rate). 1 PPS thus buys the same given volume of goods and services in all countries (see http://ec.europa.eu/eurostat).

Figure 5.1: *Median incomes and poverty thresholds in PPS, 2001*

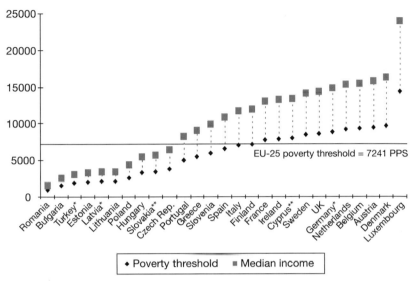

* Data relates to 2002
** Data relates to 2003
Source: Eurostat website: http://epp.eurostat.ec.europa.eu

Figure 5.2: *Relative income poverty rates* for Ireland and the accession states, 2003***

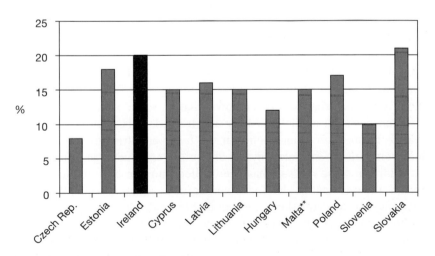

* Based on 60 per cent of median income
** Figure for Malta relates to 2000
Source: Eurostat website: http://epp.eurostat.ec.europa.eu

shows that in 2003, of the ten accession states, only Slovakia had a higher relative income poverty rate than Ireland; in the cases of Slovenia and the Czech Republic, poverty rates were considerably lower than in Ireland.

At the same time, Ireland recorded a GDP per capita that was far higher than any of the ten accession states (see Figure 5.3). In PPS terms, reflecting differences in the price levels between member states, Ireland's GDP per capita of 29000 is almost double the next highest country, Slovenia at 16500, and nearly 3.5 times that of the lowest, Latvia at 8700.

Figure 5.3: *GDP per capita in euro and PPS for Ireland and the accession states, 2003*

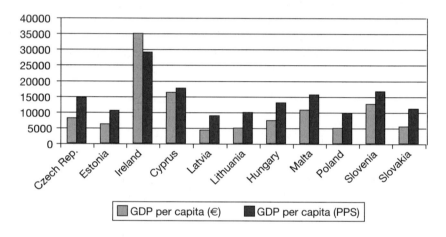

Source: Eurostat website: http://epp.eurostat.ec.europa.eu

Looking at the poverty rates for all twenty-eight member states and candidate countries, Fahey *et al.* (2005) highlight the fact that the poverty rate in such countries as Latvia is lower than in some of the more affluent EU countries such as the UK, Italy and Ireland. This, they hold, implies 'that there are more poor people in the latter countries than in Latvia'. Such comparisons indicate why the credibility and public acceptability of the relative income measure has been called into question, particularly in Ireland. Enlargement has led to the incongruous situation where the public and policy-makers are asked to accept that Ireland, which is clearly a much wealthier country than any of the ten member states that joined the EU in 2004, has, as a proportion of the population, more poor people than all but one of them.

Central to this issue is the frame of reference being used. While, it is accepted that the proportion of the population below fixed income thresholds is a 'relative' measure, the question arises: relative to what? Measuring poverty with reference to nationally defined income thresholds is useful in a national context and for the purposes of informing policy-making at national level. It is inadequate at EU level, however, particularly since enlargement from fifteen to twenty-seven member states. This enlargement has greatly increased the gap in living standards between the richest and poorest countries in the EU so that now the poverty threshold in the richer member states is equivalent to an above-average income in the poorest countries. A single adult household on 7000 PPS, for instance, would be considered to be deeply in poverty in the Netherlands, but would be well off in Estonia where 7000 PPS is more than double the median income. Fahey *et al.* (2005) elucidate the problem perfectly when they say that 'these comparisons are meaningful in terms of relativities within countries, but are in danger of inviting ridicule if presented as reflections of poverty in the everyday sense of the term'. These comparisons also give a misleading picture of the overall level of poverty and disadvantage in the EU.

Addressing this difficulty

Atkinson *et al.* (2005) suggest that one response to the problem outlined above might be to introduce an income-based indicator which would apply a common standard across the EU, i.e. setting a threshold of 60 per cent of median income across the EU, expressed in PPS. This approach answers the question posed earlier – relative to what? – by making the EU the frame of reference for the definition and measurement of poverty.

The measure would allow the presentation of the proportion of the population of each member state falling below a common EU poverty threshold. As such, those below the threshold would be considered poor relative to the prevailing standard of living across the EU as a whole. In this way, a person who is poor in Lithuania is poor in the same sense of the word as a person considered poor in the UK. It would also enable the calculation of an EU-wide poverty gap which, Atkinson *et al.* argue, would have a much more obvious interpretation than the present relative median poverty gap. For Atkinson *et al.*, this approach is justified when viewing the EU as a social entity and on the grounds that people have rights as EU citizens. There are further arguments in terms of the broader aims of the EU around the promotion of social cohesion within as well as across countries.

Fahey *et al.* (2005) make it clear that such an approach could not be a substitute for the existing set of nationally defined measures. Rather, it would involve adding a number of measures based on EU standards to the existing set of nationally based measures. Poverty measurement at the member state level should not be abandoned because data on within-country relativities in income and living standards is essential to the assessment of national poverty and socio-economic disadvantage and to the national policy-making process. It is when it comes to a wider assessment of poverty and disadvantage between or across EU member states that a broader frame of reference becomes useful and, as argued above, more meaningful.

In addition to being in line with long-established practice in academic quarters, Fahey *et al.* (2005) suggest that another reason why poverty is measured solely at the level of the member state may be due to the way social policy is dealt with in the EU. The principle of subsidiarity asserts the primacy of the role of the member state for social policy, restricting the EU's involvement to little more than a coordination function. However, Fahey (2005) holds that the EU's social policy remit in this area may not be as restrictive as it first appears due to the existence of another EU policy perspective, that of 'convergence policy'. Convergence policy is an umbrella term for a range of EU policies, including structural funds, regional policy, competition policy and the internal market, all of which aim wholly or partly to bring the poorest regions of the EU into line with the EU 'norm'.

As Fahey points out, the regional perspective measures disadvantage by reference to EU-wide thresholds based on GDP per capita, where the implication is that people are disadvantaged if the region or country they live in is economically underdeveloped by current EU standards. This approach highlights the existence of widely differing levels of disadvantage across the EU and correctly identifies the majority of recent member states as among the most disadvantaged (see Figure 5.4). This view contrasts with the current social policy perspective which defines someone as disadvantaged if they are on the margins of the society they live in, regardless of how rich or poor that society is.

The EU-wide approach to poverty measurement is intended to bring together these two equally legitimate but separately existing policy perspectives by adding a regional perspective to social policy in the EU context. This, it is argued, would facilitate commentary on European socio-economic disadvantage within a common set of measures.

Fahey *et al.* (2005) use data from the first European Quality of Life Survey (EQLS) to compare relative income poverty rates on the existing national basis and on the proposed EU median basis. They find that using national medians gives similar poverty rates for both rich and poor countries, whereas the common EU threshold produces significantly

Figure 5.4: *Disadvantage from a regional policy perspective: GDP per capita in PPS, 2003*

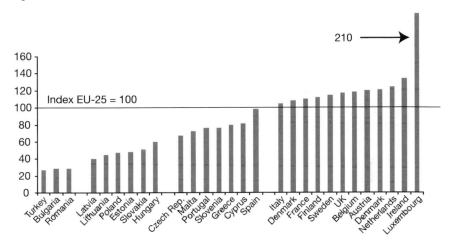

Sources: Fahey (2005) and Eurostat website: http://epp.eurostat.ec.europa.eu

Figure 5.5: *Persons below 60 per cent of national and EU median incomes*

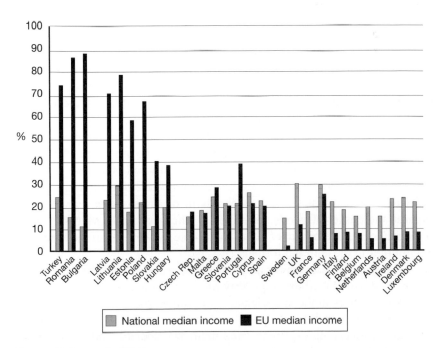

Source: Fahey *et al.* (2005)

different results, with a much larger proportion of people in the new member states and candidate countries falling below the threshold (see Figure 5.5). Focusing on the position of Ireland, the poverty rate reduces from well over 20 per cent to under 10 per cent by moving the frame of reference from the member state to the EU. In terms of ranking, Ireland's position shifts from being among those member states recording some of the highest rates of relative income poverty to being among those recording the lowest.

Using EQLS data, Fahey *et al.* also explore how people feel about their material standards of living and whether such feelings are influenced more by their relative position within their own societies or by their cross-national position in Europe. Significantly, they find that poverty measured at the EU level correlates highly with the Quality of Life Index. In contrast, national poverty measures are completely unrelated to average national levels of quality of life. The analysis suggests that the poverty rates produced by the EU median measure are a realistic reflection of the wide differences in living standards, sense of deprivation and overall quality of life found between the countries of the EU (Fahey, 2005).

Practical issues associated with adopting an EU-wide approach
Atkinson *et al.* (2005) examine the practical issues associated with adopting a broader approach to the definition and measurement of poverty in the EU. First, they address the dilemma presented by the ongoing enlargement of the EU. They propose that the measure should be based on a fixed set of member states (then twenty-five) and reviewed periodically to reflect further enlargement. This threshold would fluctuate over time in line with rises or falls in the income (expressed in PPS) of the median person in the fixed set of member states.

Second, they observe that the adoption of an EU-wide measure of relative income poverty would involve increasing the use of the PPS. They propose that, in this scenario, the distributional salience of PPS adjustments should be addressed so as to reflect consumption that is specifically relevant to those households in or at risk of poverty. This is because the basket of goods consumed by the poor is not necessarily the same as the average basket of goods, and price movements in the latter can be different to those in the former.

Looking at the case against an EU-wide approach, Atkinson *et al.* point out that the use of a common poverty line across all member states would ignore differences in the significance of goods in social functioning. With an EU-wide poverty line, it is possible that some people in richer countries who are experiencing exclusion from their own society would be missed, while substantial numbers of people in poorer states who do not feel in any way excluded from their own society would be counted. For this reason, the consensus (Atkinson *et al.*, 2005; Fahey *et al.*, 2005) favours the retention of the existing suite of Laeken indicators based around a country-specific frame of reference, but proposes that they should be complemented by an additional set of measures based on an EU-wide median threshold so as to facilitate a broader comparative analysis in an EU context.

Conclusions and implications

The relative income poverty measure, as it is currently used, has a national frame of reference; in other words, it is relative to the norms of the nation concerned. In Irish terms, the measure identifies a group of people with incomes below what could be considered 'normal' levels for Irish society and who are, as a result, unlikely to be able to participate fully in the life of that society.

Due to the availability of harmonised data at EU level, relative income poverty figures for all member states are commonly presented in league tables, ranking countries from the lowest to the highest poverty rates. This encourages the user of such statistics to make comparisons between member states. To do so, however, is not to compare like with like. Such comparisons are not based around any common standard or threshold of poverty. This has become a particular issue since the recent enlargements of the EU because the gap between the poorest and richest member states is now very much wider.

Making comparisons in a European context involves a consensus on what it is to be poor in Europe. The preceding analysis has shown that one option involves broadening the focus of the Laeken indicators to include a measure of EU-wide relative income poverty to assist the evaluation of relative performance and experience of poverty within the EU. This approach makes inter-country comparisons of poverty rates possible in an enlarged EU context. It does this by making the EU, as opposed to the member state, the frame of reference. It sets a 60 per cent median income threshold for the EU as a whole and calculates the percentage of the population in each member state falling below the threshold. Under this measure, Ireland is transformed from one of the worst performers on the basis of a straight comparison of national poverty rates to one of the best in EU terms.

There are difficulties associated with shifting the frame of reference from the member state to the EU as a whole, not least the possible loss of focus on a group of the population which, even though it is not regarded as being in poverty by an EU standard, could be experiencing disadvantage in its own society.

It can be concluded, therefore, that an EU-wide relative poverty indicator could be a useful addition to the Laeken indicators for the reporting of poverty in a comparative context. However, because poverty is defined nationally and because people are considered to be in poverty, disadvantaged or excluded relative to the immediate society in which they live, i.e. their country, national poverty rates should remain the primary focus. An EU-wide measure of relative income poverty has the potential to be a useful secondary indicator which could complement national indicators and facilitate a more meaningful comparative analysis of poverty in an EU context.

6

Assessing the Position of Vulnerable Groups

Difficulty stated

Income data as currently collected does not capture everything about an individual's or household's needs. This situation has particular implications for certain vulnerable groups such as those dependent on social welfare and for whom a range of state services and supports are available. It raises valid questions around whether income-based measures can offer a fair and true reflection of life for vulnerable groups. It is important therefore to examine the limitations of the measure when assessing the position of such groups and to explore the scope for providing the public and policy-makers with a more rounded view. In an era when increasing resources are being spent on state benefits and supports, there is also a clear need to be able to evaluate the effectiveness of such expenditure in terms of the impact it is having on the lives of the poorest in our society.

Difficulty explained and justified

From 1994 to 2001, increasing proportions of those in receipt of social welfare fell below the 60 per cent of median income poverty threshold (see Chapter 3). The percentage of the ill and disabled below the poverty threshold more than doubled from 29.5 per cent to 66.5 per cent, while the proportion of those on home duties such as lone parents rose from 20.9 per cent to 46.9 per cent. The largest increase, however, was reserved for the retired: 8.2 per cent of older people lived on incomes of less than 60 per cent of the median in 1994; by 2001, 36.9 per cent of the retired were classed as poor.

Vulnerable groups dependent on social welfare also came to make up a larger proportion of all those under the 60 per cent of median income threshold over the period. In 1994, these three groups (ill/disabled, retired and those on home duties) together made up 30 per cent of the poor, but by 2001 they accounted for 59.7 per cent of all those in poverty. As explained in Chapter 4, one of the reasons for this phenomenon is that, over the period from 1994 to 2003, increases in social welfare payments fell considerably short of the increases in median income. This trend is illustrated in Table 6.1.

Table 6.1: *Indices of income growth, 1994–2003*

	Gross average industrial earnings	Lowest social assistance payment	Contributory old age pension	Net average industrial earnings	Median equivalised disposable income
1994	100	100	100	100	100
1997	108	111	110	115	133
2000	127	129	135	147	187
2003	154	167	174	187	228

Sources: NESC (2005b) and CSO (2005b)

The period 1994 to 2003 was characterised by the relative decline in incomes of those individuals who depend on social welfare as their primary source of income vis-à-vis the rest of Irish society. Table 6.2 tracks the rates of unemployment assistance and the contributory old age pension as a percentage of the 60 per cent of median income poverty line over the period from 1994 to 2004. Both rates of payment exceeded the poverty threshold in 1994, but by 1997 they had dropped below the threshold, reaching their lowest point in 2001. Since then, the trend has been reversed somewhat, reflecting the more progressive nature of the tax and welfare changes introduced in recent budgets.

Table 6.2: *Social welfare rates as a percentage of relative income poverty, 1994–2004*

	60% of median income poverty line (€ weekly)	Unemployment assistance		Contributory old age pension	
		(€ weekly)	% of 60% median income line	(€ weekly)	% of 60% median income line
1994	76.86	77.45	100.77	90.15	117.29
1997	102.42	85.71	83.68	99.04	96.70
1998	115.80	89.52	77.31	105.39	91.01
2000	143.58	98.40	68.53	121.89	84.89
2001	164.28	108.56	66.08	134.59	81.93
2003	175.77	124.80	71.00	157.30	89.49
2004	185.51	134.80	72.66	167.30	90.18

Sources: Department of Finance (www.budget.gov.ie), CSO (2005b) and own calculations

It is interesting to note that in 2001 social welfare rates fell to their lowest value relative to the poverty threshold at the same time as the rate of relative income poverty reached its highest at 21.9 per cent (see Chapter 3). Since then, as discussed in Chapter 4, the trend for social welfare rates has been reversed. Significantly, this trend was replicated by relative income poverty rates, which fell back to 19.4 per cent in 2004. This observation echoes the finding reached by Callan *et al.* (2004a) that there is evidence of a relationship between expenditure on social security as a percentage of GDP and the rate of relative income poverty, such that every 1 per cent rise in social security as a proportion of GDP would be expected to lead to a 0.4 per cent reduction in the rate of relative income poverty.

Thus we can see that as the rates of social welfare payments as a proportion of the poverty threshold declined, the rates of relative income poverty rose. At the same time a rapidly increasing proportion of those belonging to selected vulnerable groups such as the retired and the ill and disabled fell below the poverty threshold. This may be a logical consequence of a poverty threshold that is rising more rapidly than rates of social welfare, however, it shows us that, in income terms, individuals who are dependent on social welfare are less well off relative to the rest of society today than they were in 1994 and they also face a higher risk of relative income poverty.

The figures suggest that, despite significant increases in social welfare payment rates, far exceeding the rate of price inflation and growth in gross average industrial earnings, a much higher proportion of those on social welfare are in poverty today than in 1994. How can this be? This question leads us to one of the key shortcomings of the relative income poverty measure, namely that it is based on the sole criterion of income. The income data collected in surveys such as the EU-SILC, from which poverty lines and rates are derived, do not take account of a whole range of benefits and services which make a tangible difference to people's lives. Is an analysis based solely on income too simplistic? Can it adequately capture the reality of the situation for groups such as lone parents, the retired, the long-term unemployed and the ill/disabled or is it presenting a misleading picture?

This issue is particularly relevant in the context of the large-scale public spending on benefits, services and supports. It is also important from an evidence-based policy perspective.

Addressing this difficulty

There are two ways to gain a more rounded picture of the living standards and quality of life of the most vulnerable groups in society. The first is a 'direct' approach, which seeks to place monetary values on the state services and supports that such groups receive and to factor those values into the analysis of income and the calculation of relative income poverty measures. The second approach seeks to address this issue in an 'indirect' way using budget standards and focusing primarily on expenditure.

Direct approach

As pointed out above, to focus solely on cash incomes as a measure of the resources available to households dependent on social transfers is to ignore the contribution that public services and the provision of in-kind or non-cash state benefits can make to their living standards and overall quality of life.

A host of services provided by central and local government positively impact on the lives of all those in Irish society. The fact that income-based poverty measures do not recognise the value of these services presents a problem for Irish society as a whole, but it is of particular relevance to the analysis of the position of those groups who are dependent on the state for support such as the retired, ill and disabled.

Certain public services are provided universally and so benefit lives across the income distribution. These include primary and secondary education, third level education which is now effectively subsidised by the state, public transport and library services. However, some such services are more likely to be used by the less well off in society. For example, Bramley (1997) examines data from the Breadline Britain Survey and finds that general bus services are used more often by poorer households. This finding, Bramley notes, is hardly surprising given that such households are less likely to have the use of a car. Nevertheless, it does provide confirmation of the positive contribution that certain public services make to the position of the disadvantaged, a contribution which is not reflected in poverty data based on income alone.

The state also provides a range of social care and related support services for certain vulnerable groups such as those with disabilities and the elderly. Bramley also finds these services 'pro-poor' in character.

In Ireland, the government has increased public spending significantly in real terms over recent years, particularly in the areas of health and education. Table 6.3 highlights the rapid rise of public spending from 1996 to 2003. For example, expenditure on education rose by 61 per cent and spending on health more than doubled (136.3 per cent) in real terms over the period.

It is not possible to break these figures down to show the proportion earmarked for the provision of expanded or new/additional services, or to determine who is benefiting from such services, nevertheless they do

Table 6.3: *Nominal and real (2003) gross current government expenditure, 1996–2003**

	1996	1997	1998	1999	2000	2001	2002	2003	Cumulative real growth 1996–2003
Total									
Nominal (€M)	15,464	16,858	17,985	19,738	21,994	26,328	30,225	32,661	
Real (€M)	19,361	20,794	21,664	23,390	24,675	28,163	30,920	32,661	
% real change		7.4	4.2	8.0	5.5	14.1	9.8	5.6	68.7
Health									
Nominal (€M)	2,903	3,400	3,910	4,569	5,324	6,657	7,788	8,586	
Real (€M)	3,634	4,194	4,710	5,414	5,973	7,121	7,967	8,586	
% real change		15.4	12.3	15.0	10.3	19.2	11.9	7.8	136.3
Education									
Nominal (€M)	2,666	2,999	3,105	3,361	3,716	4,219	4,808	5,376	
Real (€M)	3,338	3,699	3,740	3,983	4,169	4,513	4,919	5,376	
% real change		10.8	1.1	6.5	4.7	8.3	9.0	9.3	61.0
Social welfare									
Nominal (€M)	5,561	5,799	6,036	6,276	6,715	7,828	9,529	10,316	
Real (€M)	6,963	7,153	7,271	7,437	7,533	8,374	9,748	10,316	
% real change		2.7	1.6	2.3	1.3	11.2	16.4	5.8	48.2

* 2003 figures are estimates

Source: Lawlor and McCarthy (2003)

confirm that government spending has increased significantly over the period. They also indicate the scale of resources being channelled into the provision of health, education and social services, which benefit the lives of all those in society and in particular those on the margins, on the lowest incomes and dependent on state assistance.

The impact of the increased resources being allocated to public service provision in Ireland in recent years is not reflected by income-based poverty measures. A direct way to address this issue would be to undertake a survey to establish who uses each public service and how much use they make of the service in order to estimate a monetary amount of the benefit received by each person. This would be an onerous process.

Nolan and Russell (2001) point out that analyses conducted in the 1980s of the distributional impact of Irish public spending show that, when allocated among households on the basis of utilisation and valued at the cost of provision, Irish state services improved the relative position of those on low incomes, including those dependent on social welfare. They note that there is no reason to believe this situation has changed. However, they also make clear that while measuring the overall redistributive impact of state spending in this way is important, the difficulties in valuing the benefit to the households involved, taking into account the differences in needs and resources, are such that the task of incorporating these benefits directly into a poverty measure is 'highly problematic'.

In addition to the provision of public services themselves, the state also provides a range of in-kind benefits to social welfare recipients specifically, in particular the elderly. Nolan and Russell argue that focusing solely on income without taking into account these in-kind benefits could lead to an under-estimation of the resources available to low-income households and an over-estimation of the extent of their poverty. This is particularly likely to be the case, they hold, because of the growth in importance of such in-kind support in Ireland in recent years.

It is worthwhile attempting to assess the extent to which this may be the case, using a combination of data obtained from the EU-SILC and various administrative sources for 2006.

In-kind benefits include the Household Benefits Package, which comprises three allowances as follows:

1. The telephone allowance scheme, which provides a payment towards the costs of households' annual telephone bills. The allowance chiefly covers the standing costs relating to telephone line rental.
2. Electricity or natural gas or bottled gas allowance, only one of which is granted per household. The bottled gas refill allowance is only available for households that do not have an electricity or natural gas

supply. The electricity allowance covers normal standing charges and up to a set amount of units of electricity each year. The natural gas allowance covers normal standing or supply charges and a certain amount of natural gas kilowatt hours each year. The amount varies depending on the tariff used. The bottled gas allowance consists of a book of fifteen vouchers, which can be exchanged for cylinders of gas at retail outlets.
3.   Free TV licence.

In addition, many of those in receipt of social welfare payments are eligible for the fuel allowance. This allowance is paid to those social welfare recipients who cannot meet their fuel costs from within their own resources. It is paid weekly for 29 weeks from end-September to mid-April. Fuel allowance recipients who are living within designated smokeless fuel areas are also eligible for an additional smokeless fuel allowance. See Appendix 3 for calculations of the value of the above schemes.

A number of individual benefits are also available, including the free travel pass and the medical card. The free travel pass is available to those aged 66 or over. It permits free travel on CIÉ local and national bus and rail services and the public transport services offered by a large number of private operators in various parts of the country. The medical card entitles holders to a wide range of free medical goods and services, including free GP visits; prescribed drugs and medicines; in-patient public hospital services; out-patient services; dental, optical and aural services; medical appliances; and maternity and infant care services.

Assigning a value for the benefit obtained by the free travel pass is problematic. This is because the value of the pass depends on the use made of it. For example, Nolan and Russell point out that free travel may be of little use to those living in rural areas without public transport services and even where it is available it will be used more heavily by some people than others. They found that the information required to assess usage patterns, much less the value placed on the entitlement by different people, tends not to be available. The approach which they took to the valuation of the free travel pass was to divide the cost to the state of the provision of free travel by the number of beneficiaries to get an average annual cost per beneficiary (€81.51 in 1997).

In the case of the medical card it is not possible to indicate an annual value for each card holder. It is logical to assume that the benefit is worth proportionately more to those groups such as the ill and the elderly who are more likely to avail of medical services. Nolan and Russell also highlight a range of conceptual and methodological challenges associated with placing values on an in-kind benefit relating to healthcare such as the medical card. First, it is designed to meet a specific contingency (healthcare expenses) facing only some of the households in any given year which have the entitlement to the card. Therefore, if the cost of the free or subsidised health services supplied by the state was simply added to the household income of the relevant card holders on the basis of usage, it would imply that those who are sick are richer than those who are healthy at any given cash income level.

Another approach involves attributing a cash value to all medical cards equal to the cost of taking out an insurance policy that would provide the same benefits. The difficulty with this approach is that the value of the insurance premium could be enough to take someone over the poverty line, even though they clearly have insufficient cash income to pay for food, clothing and household bills. This prompts Nolan and Russell to conclude that such in-kind benefits do not represent command over resources in the same way that cash income does.

The approach taken by Nolan and Russell to the valuation of the in-kind benefits accruing to medical card holders is to estimate age-specific average costs of providing the service. For hospital services, the average number of nights spent in hospital by those with medical card cover was derived from a 1987 ESRI survey. The imputed values per card holder were then converted to household values using data from the 1997 LIIS, which showed that among the 44 per cent of households with at least one medical card holder the mean number of beneficiaries was 2.6. The value of the card for each household was calculated by summing the estimates for individual members. The mean imputed value worked out at €762 in 1997.

Allocating the cash values of all of the in-kind state benefits across the income distribution, Nolan and Russell find that the bottom three deciles of the income distribution, which receive only 13.4 per cent of total equivalised cash income (excluding in-kind benefits), receive 61.8 per cent of the value of the in-kind benefits. In terms of the distribution of cash-based social transfers, they find that the bottom three deciles receive 51.8 per cent of their total value. This shows that in-kind benefits are in fact more concentrated towards the bottom of the income distribution than cash-based social transfers. This finding underlines the contribution that in-kind benefits make to the lives of the poorest in society, and by extension those dependent on social welfare payments. It also provides further evidence of the importance of such in-kind benefits to obtaining a fuller picture of the position of those dependent on social welfare than is offered by income-based measures alone. Table 6.4 provides the relevant data.

Table 6.4: *Distribution of equivalised household income, in-kind benefits and cash-based social transfers, 1997*

Income decile	Equivalised household income (%)	State in-kind income (%)	Cash-based social transfers (%)
Bottom	3.6	15.9	15.5
2nd	4.6	22.2	15.7
3rd	5.2	23.7	20.6
4th	6.1	14.9	13.7
5th	7.5	9.1	11.8
6th	9.0	5.6	7.6
7th	10.7	4.7	6.9
8th	12.9	2.5	3.9
9th	16.0	0.7	2.6
Top	24.5	0.6	1.8

Source: Nolan and Russell (2001)

Table 6.5 shows that those aged over 45 receive most of the value of the in-kind benefits: 79.6 per cent in the case of the free schemes and fuel allowance and 91 per cent in the case of the medical card. Overall, it is the elderly (65+) who receive the largest share of total in-kind benefits (54.7 per cent). This is as one would expect given that most of the free schemes are aimed at the elderly and that the elderly are more likely than younger age groups to incur health problems requiring medical treatment.

Table 6.5: *Distribution of equivalised household income and in-kind benefits by age, 1997*

Age	Equivalised household income (%)	Free schemes and fuel allowance (%)	Medical card (%)	Total in-kind benefits (%)	Cash-based social transfers (%)	% in the population
<45	47.7	20.4	9.0	17.2	27.1	42.0
45–64	35.0	34.2	13.0	28.1	32.5	34.5
65+	17.3	45.4	78.0	54.7	40.4	23.5

Source: Nolan and Russell (2001)

Nolan and Russell also investigate the impact that the inclusion of in-kind benefits would have on the proportion of households falling below relative income poverty lines. They do this by adjusting household incomes to include the estimated value of the in-kind benefits and then re-calculating the relative income poverty thresholds. Table 6.6 summarises their findings. It should be pointed out that, unlike the current convention which focuses on the median, Nolan and Russell's analysis was undertaken in 2001 and therefore uses mean or average income. When the mean was used, a threshold of 50 per cent of mean income was the most commonly used relative income poverty line. It should also be noted that the focus here is on the household rather than the individual.

Table 6.6: *Households below relative income poverty lines excluding and including in-kind benefits, 1997*

	Cash income* (%)	Income + free schemes and fuel allowances (%)	Income + free schemes, fuel allowances and medical card (%)
40% of mean equivalised income	6.3	6.1	4.8
50% of mean equivalised income	22.4	17.5	14.4
60% of mean equivalised income	34.3	33.9	29.8

* Using the national equivalence scale (1.0/0.66/0.33)
Source: Nolan and Russell (2001)

Table 6.6 shows that the inclusion of the free schemes and fuel allowances has a major impact on household poverty levels using a 50 per cent of mean income line, with the rate dropping from 22.4 per cent to 17.5 per cent. However, their inclusion has relatively little impact on the 40 per cent and 60 per cent thresholds. When the medical card is added, poverty levels fall further at the 50 per cent level to 14.4 per cent. The inclusion of the medical card also makes an impact on poverty levels at the 40 per cent and 60 per cent thresholds, which drop from 6.1 per cent to 4.8 per cent and from 33.9 per cent to 29.8 per cent respectively.

Table 6.7 presents a disaggregated picture focusing on the impact of the inclusion of in-kind benefits on the poverty rates for key groups in society. It shows once again that it is the vulnerable groups in society who are relying on cash-based social welfare payments that benefit most from the in-kind benefits. The poverty rates for these groups – the unemployed, the ill/disabled, the retired and those on home duties (including carers and lone parents) – are all reduced when values for the in-kind benefits are included.

In the case of the retired and those on home duties, poverty levels fall considerably when in-kind benefits are included, from 23.3 per cent to 7.6

Table 6.7: *Population below 50 per cent of mean income when in-kind benefits are excluded and included by labour force status, 1997*

Labour force status of household reference person	Cash incomes*		Cash incomes + in-kind benefits	
	% below the 50% of mean income line	*Composition of all those below the 50% of mean income line*	*% below the 50% of mean income line*	*Composition of all those below the 50% of mean income line*
Employed	4.0	7.2	4.1	11.8
Self-employed	17.1	6.1	14.8	8.3
Farmer	16.3	4.9	14.2	6.7
Unemployed	54.9	18.6	48.1	25.6
Ill/disabled	60.4	9.0	54.3	12.7
Retired	23.3	17.6	7.6	9.0
Home duties	48.6	35.2	20.9	23.8
All	22.3	100.0	14.2	100.0

* Using the national equivalence scale (1.0/0.66/0.33)
Source: Nolan and Russell (2001)

per cent and 48.6 per cent to 20.9 per cent respectively. These categories also make up much less of the total number of those in poverty when in-kind benefits are taken into account. When the benefits are excluded, these two groups accounted for over one-half (52.8 per cent) of all those in poverty; when the benefits are included, they account for less than one-third (31.8 per cent). The retired benefited proportionately more than other groups from in-kind benefits, which is as one might expect given that many of the free schemes are directed at the elderly and that the elderly are more likely to need to avail of medical services. This provides further evidence to suggest that measures based solely on income do not fully capture the reality of the situation of the most vulnerable in our society, many of whom are receiving assistance from the state.

The introduction of the EU-SILC in 2003 provides the context for presenting an up-to-date analysis of the value of in-kind benefits to social welfare recipients and the impact on the incidence of poverty among these groups. Relative income poverty statistics now take account of the following in-kind state benefits: telephone allowance, electricity allowance, natural gas allowance, free bottled gas allowance, fuel allowance and smokeless fuel allowance.

Table 6.8 shows the position in 2005/6 in relation to each of the main in-kind benefits, providing details as to who is eligible and the annual value of the benefit in each case. It shows that these benefits were worth €1,309.20 per year or €25.18 per week to recipients. Appendix 3 provides more detail on each of the benefits and the calculation of current values. The table does not show certain other benefits such as waivers from local authority waste charges. In some local authority areas, low-income households can avail of a waiver on waste charges by private refuse operators and local authorities. However, currently these waivers vary greatly from region to region and in some areas they are not available at all.

It will be noted from Table 6.8 that the Household Benefits Package and the free travel pass primarily benefit the retired and the ill/disabled – two of the groups identified in the data analysis earlier as facing particularly high risks of relative income poverty. The fuel and smokeless fuel allowances and the medical card are more widely available to different categories of social welfare recipients.

The free travel pass and the medical card continue to be excluded from the analysis of income in the EU-SILC. However, the survey includes one question which asks respondents who possess a free travel pass to estimate how much they have saved in public transport fares in the last four weeks as a result of using the pass. It is possible to annualise the amounts provided by respondents to obtain an overall subjective value for the benefit of the free travel pass. When this is done using data from the 2004 EU-SILC, it shows that the average annualised value for the free travel pass in 2004 was €109.02.

The reliability issues associated with data obtained from such a subjective question explain why these values are not currently included in the analysis of income. First, respondents may not have an accurate recollection of the extent to which they used public transport in the last four weeks. Second, they may not have sufficient information as to bus or train fares for the travel they undertook which could prompt them to take a guess as to the amount saved. Third, the overall average value obtained when aggregating all of the responses to this question tends to be skewed by a small number of particularly high values.

Although the figure obtained from the 2004 EU-SILC data provides a useful indicative value for the purposes of this analysis, it is important to recognise that the pass is likely to have a 'pro-poor' distribution, with those pensioners on low incomes and without cars or alternative transport using the pass more than those with cars. Accordingly, the value of €109.02 may understate the value to those at the bottom of the income distribution who depend on the state pension as their primary source of income.

The EU-SILC does not ask respondents to impute a value for the medical costs saved as a result of having the medical card. This is because respondents are unlikely to know the costs in many cases. Therefore, Table 6.8 includes a figure for the costs of administering the scheme to each

Table 6.8: *The main in-kind benefits available to social welfare recipients, 2005/2006*

State benefit	Who is eligible	Yearly value*
Telephone allowance**	• All those aged over 70 • Those aged between 66 and 69 who pass a means test • Those aged under 66 who are disabled/incapacitated	€296.40
Free TV licence**	As above	€155.00
Electricity, natural gas or bottled gas allowance**	As above	€338.70†
Fuel allowance**	Those in receipt of social welfare payments (including contributory pensions) and those taking part in educational or employment schemes, who satisfy a means test	€406.00 or €519.10 incl. smokeless fuel allowance
	Total value per year††	€1309.20
	Total value per week††	€25.18
Free travel scheme	• Those aged 66 and over • Those aged under 66 who are disabled/incapacitated	€109.02
Medical card	• All persons over 70 years of age • Those aged 69 and under whose income from employment is below a certain threshold • Those in receipt of certain social welfare payments with no other form of income	N/A But in terms of the *costs* of the scheme an overall payment per eligible person of €809.48 was made in 2003

* Values relate to 2005 with the exception of the fuel allowance figure which is based on the rate of €14 per week applicable from 1 January 2006, and the free travel pass which is based on 2004 EU-SILC data
** Allowance payable on a per household basis
† The figure quoted relates to the value of the electricity allowance; the gas allowances confer similar values (Nolan and Russell, 2001)
†† Based on inclusion of the smokeless fuel allowance
Sources: CSO, www.oasis.gov.ie, www.cie, www.welfare.ie and General Medical Services (Payments) Board (2004)

eligible person as a proxy value for this benefit. In 2003, these costs worked out at €809.48 per eligible person.

It is also important to understand the impact these in-kind benefits have on the rates of relative income poverty. For the purposes of this exercise, a breakdown of EU-SILC data was obtained showing relative income poverty rates for 2003 and 2004 exclusive of the free schemes listed above. Overall poverty rates, exclusive and inclusive of the free schemes, are set out in Table 6.9. This data shows that in 2004, for example, the overall proportion of the population falling below the 60 per cent of median income poverty threshold was some 2 per cent lower, at 19.4 per cent, than it would otherwise have been if the free schemes were not taken into account. In other words, if such benefits were still excluded from the analysis (as they were until 2001) the poverty rate for 2004 would be 21.4 per cent. This gives an insight into the poverty-reducing impact of in-kind benefits.

Table 6.9: *Impact of in-kind benefits* on relative income poverty rates, 2003 and 2004*

	% below the 60% of median income threshold	
	2003	*2004*
Excluding in-kind benefits	21.2	21.4
Including in-kind benefits	19.7	19.4
Change	−1.5	−2.0

* In-kind benefits here include: telephone allowance, electricity allowance, natural gas allowance, free bottled gas allowance, fuel allowance and smokeless fuel allowance; but exclude the free travel pass and the medical card
Source: EU-SILC data decomposition obtained from the CSO

Using EU-SILC data it is also possible to examine the impact of the free schemes on particular groups in society and to identify the main beneficiaries. Table 6.10 shows clearly that the free schemes have the biggest impact on those on home duties and the retired (many of whom are likely to be dependent on social welfare) with poverty rates for these groups falling from 39.1 per cent to 32.1 per cent and 35.1 per cent to 26.1 per cent respectively.

The introduction of the EU-SILC has led to the inclusion of a number of in-kind benefits in the analysis of poverty, which in turn produced a poverty rate in 2004 some 2 per cent lower than would have been the case were they excluded. However, a number of important in-kind benefits which make a difference to the living standards and quality of life of social

Table 6.10: *Impact of free schemes on relative income poverty rates by principal economic status, 2004*

| | % below the 60% of median income threshold | | Change |
	Excluding free schemes	Including free schemes	
At work	7.2	7.0	–0.2
Unemployed	38.1	37.2	–0.9
Student	24.0	23.6	–0.4
Home duties	39.0	32.1	–6.9
Retired	35.1	26.1	–9.0
Ill/disabled	52.4	47.3	–5.1
Children under 16	22.1	21.9	–0.2
Other	55.5	52.3	–3.2
All	21.4	19.4	–2.0

Source: EU-SILC data decomposition provided following request to the CSO

welfare recipients are still not taken into account. These include the free travel pass and the medical card.

There are also significant benefits accruing to those in local authority housing who are paying below market rents. This is effectively an implicit subsidy from the state. Housing is an important yet complex issue to analyse and the problems it poses are assessed in detail in Chapter 7.

The EU-SILC does contain a range of questions relating to the free travel pass, the medical card and rental costs, which provide useful additional information. However, they do not resolve all of the difficulties associated with valuing public services and in-kind benefits and therefore have not yet been incorporated into the analysis.

A key issue with the direct survey approach to estimating the value of public services and in-kind benefits is the poor level and quality of information held by respondents as to their use and the value of such services. Therefore services, in-kind benefits and subsidies provided by the state and making a tangible difference to the lives of social welfare recipients are not fully reflected in an income-based analysis of poverty. This prompts Bradshaw (2004) to conclude that relative income poverty statistics do not resonate with the general public, commentators and policy-makers because they do not tell them what level of living people below the relative income poverty threshold have. The analysis above indicates the scale of the conceptual and methodological challenges associated with a direct approach when trying to arrive at meaningful values for public services, state subsidies and in-kind benefits.

Indirect approach

If poverty figures are expected to provide a true reflection of the living standards of vulnerable groups, families and individuals, then values for the full range of supports, subsidies and benefits they receive are required to be taken into account. Given the issues and difficulties associated with the relative income poverty measure discussed above, alternative approaches are worth considering.

The indirect approach shifts the emphasis from an analysis based on income to one based on expenditure. Atkinson (1974), while accepting income as the correct measure, argues that expenditure may represent a better indicator of 'true' income. This approach involves examining expenditure on goods and services as a means of determining what an adequate level of income should be and is known as the budget standards method.

Bradshaw (1993) defines a budget standard as 'a specified basket of goods and services which, when priced, can represent a particular standard of living'. The budget standards approach can indirectly deal with the issue of in-kind benefits received and public services availed of by those on social welfare. This is because it seeks to establish how much income a household in particular circumstances (for example, a household headed by an adult on unemployment assistance with three children) requires on a weekly basis. Implicit in this approach is that the expenditure that the household incurs (and thereby the income it requires) is reduced by the extent of the state supports, services and in-kind benefits it is entitled to receive. The income that a household requires is therefore net of the value of these supports, services and benefits.

In other words, the budget standards approach looks at how much income a given household needs to cover the expenditure it is required to make to achieve a certain standard of living, after all services and in-kind benefits are taken into account. For example, if the members of Household A do not hold a free travel pass, then a reasonable provision would have to be made in that household's budget for bus and train fares. If, on the other hand, the members of Household B do possess a free travel pass, then no expenditure provision needs to be made to cover bus and train fares and, therefore, no income is required to cover such costs. Assuming that they are in similar households, the income required to achieve a given standard of living will be higher for Household A than for Household B. The amount by which Household A's budget requirement (and hence income requirement) exceeds that of Household B indicates the value of the free travel pass held by Household B.

There are an infinite number of possible budgets which could be priced depending on the living standard one is seeking to define. For example, in the 1990s, the Family Budget Unit at the University of York defined two budgets: a 'low cost but acceptable' (LCA) budget that represents the threshold below which good health, social integration and satisfactory standards of child development are at risk; and a 'modest but adequate' (MBA) budget that is well above the requirements for survival but well below the levels of luxury (Bradshaw, 1993).

Drawing on the work of the Family Budget Unit, the Vincentian Partnership for Social Justice applied the budget standards approach in Ireland in 2004. The study (MacMahon *et al.,* 2004) set out to provide detailed information on the actual cost of an LCA budget, as defined above, for different income scenarios within three Irish household types, many of which depend on social welfare cash transfers and had been identified by a previous study by the Partnership in 2000 as being most at risk of poverty. The income scenarios covered by the study are:

1. Lone parent with two children (aged 4 and 10)
    (a) in receipt of social welfare
    (b) on the national minimum wage.
2. Couple with two children (aged 4 and 10)
    (a) in receipt of social welfare
    (b) on the national minimum wage
    (c) participating in the Local Authority Tenant Purchase Scheme.
3. Pensioner couple (who own their own home outright)
    (a) in receipt of a contributory pension (and qualified adult allowance)
    (b) in receipt of a non-contributory pension (and qualified adult allowance)
    (c) in receipt of income from a private pension.

Focusing on those families depending on social welfare as their main income source within each of the three household types, MacMahon *et al.* sought to compare the income required to meet budgeted expenditure with the amount of income each household is currently entitled to in terms of social welfare payments from the state. This comparison permitted conclusions to be reached as to the adequacy of existing payment rates.

The LCA budget was considered appropriate because it resonates closely with the definition of poverty set out in the National Anti-Poverty Strategy (NAPS). The *Report of the Commission on Social Welfare* (1986) provided a further context in terms of its recommendation that, to be adequate, social welfare payments 'must prevent poverty, and in our view poverty must be judged in the light of actual standards of living in contemporary Irish society'. Therefore, MacMahon *et al.*'s application of the LCA budget standard could be regarded as an attempt to determine the cost of avoiding poverty as set out in the NAPS and of allowing a standard of living that would meet basic physical, social and psychological needs. It would involve indicating how low-income families actually spend their money as well as showing how their money should be spent in order to have a socially inclusive lifestyle.

The LCA budget standards developed consist of a number of component budgets relating to food, clothing, personal care, household goods, household services, leisure (social inclusion items and activities), housing (including rent, maintenance and waste collection), fuel, transport (public and private), healthcare, educational costs, employment-related expenses (including childcare), costs of seeking employment and charitable donations. A total of 1,200 items were priced. The LCA budget does not make provision for unexpected demands on income or for debt and loan repayments.

In applying the LCA budget to the Irish situation, the following structure was put in place to ensure the reliability and validity of the process. A research advisory committee was established consisting of the key agencies and non-governmental organisations that deal with the three household types. Expert advice was sought from a number of quarters including the University of York. Finally, focus groups were established for each household type to examine each of the component items of the budget.

Table 6.11 summarises the key findings in respect of the six social welfare dependent household scenarios explored by the study. There are a number of points to note about the data. First, the LCA budget makes no provision for unexpected expenditure. However, MacMahon *et al.* argue that such expenditure can cause major problems for families dependent on a low income. For this reason, they surveyed members of the Money Advice and Budgeting Service (MABS) and, based on their responses, arrived at a figure of €30 per week to cover the expenses associated with unforeseen eventualities. This figure was added to each of the LCA budgets subsequently.

Second, the budgets take full account of in-kind benefits such as the medical card, the free travel pass and the Household Benefits Package. The budgets for the lone parent and the two adult with children households also take into account the implicit subsidy associated with renting a house from the local authority in that the provision made for housing costs is that much less than would otherwise be the case. The pensioner couple in all four scenarios laid out in the table are assumed to be owner-occupiers with no rent/mortgage costs.

Table 6.11: *LCA budgets for selected households compared with income from social welfare, August 2004*

Household type and income scenario	Total LCA budget costs (€ weekly)	LCA + €30 provision for unexpected expenses (€ weekly)	Total cash income from the state (€ weekly)	Income surplus or (shortfall) (€ weekly)
Lone parent and two children dependent on social welfare (no car)	259.29	289.29	235.67	(53.62)
Two adults and two children in receipt of unemployment benefit (no car)	326.36	356.36	320.07	(36.29)
Couple in receipt of contributory pension (no car)	222.99	252.99	316.75	63.76
Couple in receipt of contributory pension (own car)	302.30	332.30	316.75	(15.55)
Couple in receipt of non-contributory pension (no car)	210.97	240.97	276.05	35.08
Couple in receipt of non-contributory pension (own car)	290.28	320.28	276.05	(44.23)

Source: MacMahon *et al.* (2004)

MacMahon *et al.* find, as shown in Table 6.11, that the level of income support from the state was insufficient to cover the LCA budget for a lone parent with two children, for a couple with two children in receipt of unemployment benefit and for a car-owning couple in receipt of the non-contributory pension. The shortfall was even greater when allowance was made for unexpected expenses of €30 per week and the couple in receipt of the contributory pension who owned a car also had insufficient income in this scenario.

Given that increasing numbers of social welfare groups are falling below the 60 per cent of median income line, it is useful to explore how the LCA budgets for the six household types compare to the poverty threshold for each. To calculate the euro threshold for each of the three household types, the equivalised household size for each is obtained using the national equivalence scale (see Chapter 2) and this is then multiplied by the weekly euro value of the 60 per cent median income threshold (€185.51 in 2004). Table 6.12 shows these calculations and the resulting poverty threshold for each household.

Table 6.12: *Calculation of household poverty thresholds, 2004*

Household type	60% of median income threshold (€ weekly)	Equivalent household size	Household poverty threshold at the 60% of median income level (€ weekly)
Lone parent and two children (aged 4 and 10)	185.51	1.66 (1.00+0.33+0.33)	307.95
Two adults and two children (aged 4 and 10) on unemployment benefit	185.51	2.32 (1.00+0.66+0.33+0.33)	430.38
Pensioner couple*	185.51	1.66 (1.00+0.66)	307.95

* This applies to any of the four pensioner scenarios given in Table 6.11

Figure 6.1 shows how the LCA budget (without provision for unexpected expenses) and the social welfare income to which each household type was entitled compare with the 60 per cent of median income threshold for each household in 2004. The key observation is that the LCA budget is less than the relative income poverty threshold in the case of all six household scenarios. This suggests that the relative income poverty threshold may be overstating the amount of income that such households require to obtain a standard of living that ensures 'good health, social integration and satisfactory standards of child development' and hence to avoid poverty and social exclusion as we understand and define them. It is also noteworthy that only pensioner couples in receipt of the contributory pension have a social welfare income that exceeds these relative income poverty thresholds.

Figure 6.2 shows the results when the €30 per week provision for unexpected expenses is added to the LCA budget figures. In four of the six cases the relative income poverty threshold continues to exceed the LCA budget. It is only in the case of the pensioner couples with cars that the LCA budget is higher than the relative income poverty threshold.

Figure 6.1: *LCA budgets, social welfare incomes and poverty thresholds for six household scenarios, 2004*

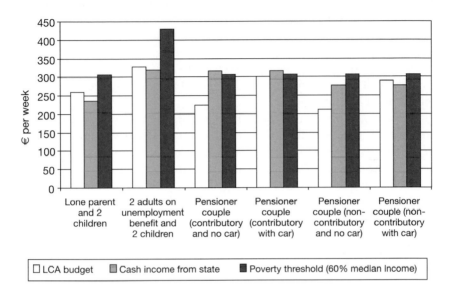

Figure 6.2: *LCA budgets including provision for unexpected expenses and the poverty threshold for six household scenarios, 2004*

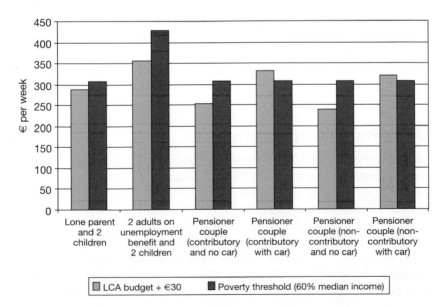

This analysis provides further evidence that relative income poverty figures may indeed be giving a misleading impression of the position of groups on social welfare. The analysis based on budget standards shows that those households that are commonly regarded as facing the highest risks require an income less than the relative income poverty threshold to achieve a low cost but acceptable standard of living. As the LCA budget takes into account all of the free services, in-kind benefits, subsidies and supports that are available to each household type, it may provide a better reflection of 'true income'.

The analysis above illustrates how a budget standards approach can enhance our understanding of the expenditure needs of vulnerable groups in our society. Relative income poverty thresholds, on the other hand, bear no explicit relationship to the actual income that is required by households to attain a specified standard of living. They say nothing about the amount of income required for a household to get by. Budget standards also facilitate an assessment as to the adequacy of social welfare payment rates. It is possible, for example, to establish whether or not they are sufficient to provide a low cost but acceptable living standard. MacMahon *et al.* (2004) have shown, in the case of a lone parent with two children and a household with two adults and two children depending on unemployment benefit, that the income support provided by the state in 2004 after services, subsidies and in-kind benefits were taken into account, was insufficient to achieve a low cost but acceptable standard of living for the members of those households.

There is a case for exploring how the budget standards method could usefully enhance the policy-making process in Ireland. For example, one option might be to build on the work of the Vincentian Partnership for Social Justice by drawing up budget standards for a range of household scenarios for the main vulnerable groups living on the margins of Irish society.

Conclusions and implications

Income-based measures have limitations. They do not capture the totality of the resources at the disposal of an individual or a household and which contribute to that person's or household's standard of living. This is a particular issue for low-income vulnerable groups in society, many of whom depend on social welfare as their main source of income. These groups also receive a range of other state benefits, supports and services, many of which are not taken into account by income-based poverty measures. Income-based measures showed increasing proportions of vulnerable groups such as lone parents, the ill/disabled, the retired and the unemployed falling into poverty during the period 1994 to 2001. However, the fact that such groups benefit from a range of state-provided or subsidised supports was not included in the analysis and leads the policy-maker to question the value and validity of these trends.

An exploration of a direct approach to addressing this issue, which involved factoring these values into the analysis of income, highlighted the difficulties associated with estimating the value of public services to such vulnerable groups. For example, to adopt such an approach fully would involve an onerous audit of public service usage before attempting to assign valuations to households which could then be factored into the analysis of income. It is possible, however, to come up with values for a number of the in-kind benefits and supports that certain vulnerable groups are eligible to receive. The exercise carried out here showed that the Household Benefits Package and fuel allowances, for example, were worth up to €1,309.20 per year or €25.18 per week for recipients, who are primarily elderly.

In view of the scale of the resources committed to the provision of public services, however, it is suggested that this is one area where further work could usefully be done. Such work could establish whether there is a viable and cost-effective way to incorporate into the system of poverty measurement some means of gauging the beneficial impact of public services generally but particularly those which are focused on improving the situation of groups dependent on the state for assistance and facing an above-average risk of poverty.

The introduction of the EU-SILC has led to the inclusion of a number of these in-kind benefits in the analysis of poverty. Analysis has shown that their inclusion directly results in a drop in the relative income poverty rate by two percentage points. At the disaggregated level in particular, the inclusion of the in-kind benefits has the effect of reducing poverty levels for a number of social welfare groups who receive these benefits, most notably the retired (35.1 per cent to 26.1 per cent). This finding provides evidence of the effectiveness of public expenditure on in-kind benefits in terms of improving the circumstances of those on the lowest incomes and reducing poverty.

Therefore, it is possible to use a direct valuation approach to incorporate certain benefits into the analysis of income but others such as the free travel pass and the medical card continue to be problematic. Given these problems, it can be concluded that the relative income poverty measure does not provide a full picture of the situation of those on lowest incomes who receive a range of state benefits and supports. As such, the validity and value of relative income poverty data to the policy-maker may also be legitimately questioned.

This finding prompted the consideration of an indirect approach to addressing the difficulty posed by the need to incorporate state services, in-kind benefits and supports into the measurement of poverty based on budget standards. This approach is intended primarily to address issues of income adequacy by determining how much income a particular household requires, given the expenditure it must make to achieve a very basic standard of living. This approach effectively incorporates the value of state benefits and subsidies into the analysis because the income required by a household receiving these benefits will be lower than the income required by a similar household that has to pay for such goods and services.

Drawing on the work of the Vincentian Partnership for Social Justice (MacMahon *et al.*, 2004), which provides a useful illustration of how budget standards could be applied in an Irish context, this chapter examined the position of a number of social welfare household types in 2004. A lone parent with two children and an unemployed couple with two children did not receive sufficient weekly income from the state to meet the expenditure required to achieve a low cost but acceptable standard of living. While a pensioner couple with no car enjoyed a modest weekly income surplus, this reverted to a deficit for those owning a car.

Comparing the LCA budgets from this study with the relative income poverty thresholds for each of these household types, including a provision for unexpected expenditure of €30 per week, the threshold continued to exceed the income required for each of the budgets with the exception of car-owning pensioners who require an income that is slightly higher than the threshold to be sure of a low cost but acceptable living standard.

This analysis reinforces the assertion that relative income poverty thresholds do not necessarily bear any explicit relationship to the actual income that is required by households to achieve a certain standard of living. It suggests that when all in-kind benefits and other state supports are factored into the analysis, certain social welfare households can achieve an acceptable standard of living on an income which is below the poverty threshold.

On this basis, it could be argued that the relative income poverty measure overstates poverty in Ireland, particularly for key social welfare groups such as the elderly, who are shown to be increasingly at risk of poverty. Equally, it could be argued that poverty thresholds framed around the objectively defined needs set out in budget standards for selected vulnerable household types may be more meaningful to the policy-maker and resonate more closely with the public. For example, if a household has an income less than the amount required for that household type to achieve a low cost but acceptable living standard, then the members of that household could reasonably be assumed to be living in poverty.

As well as providing the potential for valuable insight into the needs of low-income households, the budget standards approach also facilitates an assessment of the adequacy of social welfare payment rates. For example, Conniffe *et al.* (1998) find that this approach 'has clear value in demonstrating what a given level of money can and cannot buy at a particular point in time, and this can be valuable information to policy-makers and the wider public in assessing the adequacy of income support levels'. Using this approach, MacMahon *et al.* (2004) have shown social welfare payment rates to be deficient in certain cases.

In conclusion, there is a case for examining the potential for mainstreaming a limited budget standards exercise in respect of a number of particularly vulnerable household types. This could inform policy on social welfare and child income support rates. It would also provide a means of tracking the benefit of services to these vulnerable groups. The work by the Vincentian Partnership for Social Justice provides a certain basis on which to build. Specifically, the scope for 'piggy-backing' on existing household surveys could be investigated. Such budgets could perhaps be uprated annually to reflect changes in the Consumer Price Index, and reformulated periodically, say every five years to coincide with the periodic rebasing of the Consumer Price Index itself in the Household Budget Survey.

7

Housing Cost Considerations

Difficulty stated

A further shortcoming of the relative income poverty measure is that it fails to take account of housing expenditure, the benefit of outright ownership of housing or the reduced rent paid by those in local authority accommodation. This is a notable omission in the Irish context given the significance of housing costs and benefits and the concern over housing affordability.

Difficulty explained and justified

The total number of dwellings in Ireland almost doubled from 662,600 in 1946 to 1,279,600 in 2002. The rate of home-ownership rose steadily from 52.6 per cent to 77.4 per cent over the same period. A notable urban/rural divide in home-ownership in the 1940s (with over 69 per cent of rural dwellers owning their own homes compared to just 23.2 per cent of urban dwellers) had been largely bridged by 2002. A striking feature of housing tenure over the period is the decline in the social housing sector from 18.4 per cent of all dwellings to 6.8 per cent. The private rented sector also declined over much of the period but has recovered somewhat in recent years.

Recent years have seen exponential growth in average Irish house prices. In March 1996, for example, the average price of a house in Ireland was €75,169. By March 2005, it had increased by 241 per cent to €256,690. The price of a new house nationally was over three times the average disposable income in 1996, rising to 4.1 times the average disposable earnings by 2002. The corresponding figures for Dublin were approximately 3.5 in 1996 and 5.2 in 2002 (Fahey *et al.*, 2004a). The impact of these rapid increases was mitigated to some extent by a fall in interest rates during the 1990s to historically low levels.

The Department of the Environment, Heritage and Local Government maintains an index of housing affordability based on a household with one person earning the average non-industrial wage and another earning the average industrial wage. The 2004 mortgage outgoings are based on a twenty-year mortgage, a 3.25 per cent interest rate and an average national house price of €249,198 (Government of Ireland, 2005). Affordability is measured by reference to the costs of servicing a mortgage and therefore factors into the analysis the impact of rises and falls in interest rates. It also takes into account the evolution in household disposable income. Figure 7.1 shows how this index evolved over the period from 1988 to 2004. Specifically, it shows that housing affordability deteriorated sharply between 1988 and 1993 with the mortgage outgoings of a typical household rising from 21 per cent of disposable income in 1988 to close to 30 per cent in 1993. Between 1993 and 1995, there was a short-lived but significant improvement in affordability. Since 1995, housing affordability has once again deteriorated with mortgage outgoings as a percentage of household disposable income rising steadily from under 21 per cent, reaching 27 per cent in 2000 and then falling back to 25 per cent in 2004.

Overall, Figure 7.1 shows that although housing was less affordable in 2004 than in the mid-1990s, it was more affordable in 2004 than in the early 1990s. This is despite the phenomenal growth in house prices since the mid-1990s. The reasons why housing was more affordable in 2004 than in the early 1990s include the availability of much lower interest rates and much higher levels of household disposable income. The decline in affordability since the mid-1990s shows that the beneficial impact of these two factors has been outweighed by house price increases.

Figure 7.1: *Housing affordability (mortgage payments as a percentage of net income), 1988–2004*

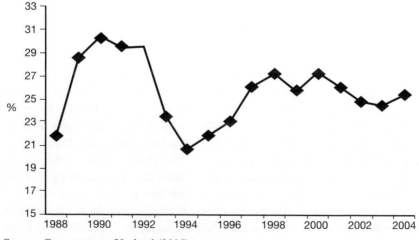

Source: Government of Ireland (2005)

In 2003, 61.8 per cent of all owner-occupiers had no loan or mortgage payments. As such, those with loans or mortgages accounted for around one in three of all owner-occupiers (CSO, 2005d). Those owner-occupiers with no mortgage payments tend to be concentrated in the 55-plus age groups. Table 7.1 shows that, whereas only 6.2 per cent of those under 35 years owned a house without mortgage payments in 2000, almost 81 per cent of those aged 65 to 74 owned their house outright.

Table 7.1: *Owner-occupied households with and without mortgages as a percentage of all households by age, 2000*

Age of household reference person	Owner-occupied households (%)	Owner-occupied households with a mortgage (%)	Owner-occupied households without a mortgage (%)
Under 35	53.2	47.0	6.2
35–44	83.0	65.5	16.5
45–54	87.1	48.1	39.0
55–64	86.0	24.7	60.3
65–74	92.5	11.7	80.8
74 and over	81.9	4.5	77.4

Source: Fahey *et al.* (2004a)

Table 7.1 confirms that the vast majority of Irish pensioners own their own homes outright and consequently are not faced with housing expenditure in terms of mortgage or rental payments. The situation is very different for those in the younger age categories. Fahey *et al.* (2004a) analyse rent and mortgage expenditure by 'family lifecycle stage' using micro-data from the 1994/1995 and 1999/2000 Household Budget Surveys. They find that, for those in the early stages of family formation, expenditure on mortgages/rent as a share of total household expenditure increased between 1994/1995 and 1999/2000. Also, such expenditure was a good deal higher for these groups than for those in the middle and later stages of the lifecycle. Housing expenditure in 1999/2000 accounted for 18.4 per cent of total expenditure for young single households and 15 per cent of total expenditure for households with a child aged four or less. In contrast, a retired couple could expect to face costs amounting to just 2 per cent of total household expenditure.

Table 7.2 compares the position of the four key housing tenure groups over the period from 1973 to 2000: outright homeowners (who are most likely to be in or close to retirement), owner-occupiers with a mortgage, those renting from a local authority (social renters) and those renting from private sector landlords. In the case of the outright homeowners, the table simply highlights that they faced no rental/mortgage expenditure. Homeowners with mortgages on the other hand have seen their mortgage costs rise almost threefold from €28.71 per week in 1973 (adjusted to 2000 prices) to €73.19 per week in 2000. Mortgage payments accounted for 9.6 per cent of household expenditure in 2000 compared to 7.1 per cent in 1973.

In sharp contrast to the situation for mortgage holders, those renting housing from local authorities faced much lower costs at €22.69 per week in 2000 and, significantly, these costs have remained relatively stable over the period, rising by only 5 per cent from €21.55 in 1973. Therefore, rental costs as a percentage of total household expenditure for this group is the same in 2000, at 7.4 per cent, as it was in 1973.

The most striking observation from Table 7.2 relates to the position of those renting in the private sector. Here rents have soared by 259 per cent in real terms from €35.14 per week in 1973 to €126.30 per week in 2000. As a percentage of total household expenditure, they have risen from 12.5 per cent to 21 per cent over the period. Figure 7.2 summarises these findings. It highlights the contrast between two tenure groups who face low or no housing expenditures and two tenure groups facing large housing expenditures which have been rising steeply in real terms. The former are outright homeowners (who are in the main those in or close to retirement) and those renting from local authorities (many of whom will be social welfare dependents). The latter are mortgage-holders (mainly in the early stages of family formation) and those renting in the private sector.

The position for mortgage-holders, as indicated by the percentage of their total household expenditure accounted for by mortgage payments,

Figure 7.2: *Evolution of weekly housing expenditure by tenure category, 1973–2000*

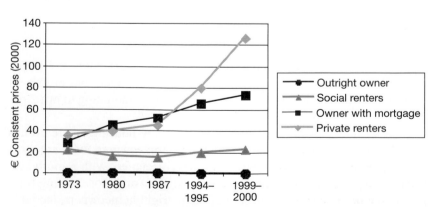

Table 7.2: *Trends in housing expenditure indicators by tenure, 1973–2000**

	1973	1980	1987	1994/ 1995	1999/ 2000	% change 1973– 2000
Outright owner						
Mortgage payments (€)	0.00	0.00	0.00	0.00	0.00	0
Total household expenditure (€)	339.61	379.89	352.87	378.77	480.41	41
Mortgage as % of total	0.00	0.00	0.00	0.00	0.00	0
Total equivalised** household expenditure (€)	176.32	205.42	201.39	223.97	293.46	66
Owner with mortgage						
Mortgage payments (€)	28.71	45.44	51.78	65.19	73.19	157
Total household expenditure (€)	404.10	577.12	526.59	625.89	767.40	90
Mortgage as % of total	7.10	7.90	9.80	10.40	9.60	35
Total equivalised** household expenditure (€)	189.24	274.82	258.49	341.92	395.76	109
Social renters						
Rent (€)	21.55	15.31	14.63	19.10	22.69	5
Total household expenditure (€)	289.31	326.72	252.06	252.63	306.99	6
Rent as % of total	7.40	4.70	5.80	7.60	7.40	0
Total equivalised** household expenditure (€)	130.83	156.47	127.80	136.21	172.97	32
Private renters						
Rent (€)	35.14	39.48	45.25	80.26	126.30	259
Total household expenditure (€)	280.54	372.00	360.98	423.72	601.93	115
Rent as % of total	12.50	10.60	12.50	18.90	21.00	68
Total equivalised** household expenditure (€)	161.43	240.12	230.62	270.70	369.07	129

* Prices are expressed in constant 2000 terms
** Equivalence scale used = the square root of household size
Source: Fahey *et al.* (2004a)

has deteriorated over the period but not enormously. However, Fahey *et al.* (2004a) observe the opening of a large gap between the burden of housing expenditures for mortgage purchasers and for private renters, concluding that the marked deterioration in the position of the latter group constitutes one of the most serious affordability problems in the Irish housing system. Taking expenditures on rent or mortgage payments exceeding 35 per cent of household expenditure as an indicator of housing affordability problems, they show that 20 per cent of private renters had such problems in 1999/2000 whereas only 1 per cent of mortgage-holders were in this position.

Fahey *et al.* point out that, at a given level of income, a household which must spend 25 per cent of its income on rent or mortgage payments is clearly in a very different situation to the outright homeowner with no such payments. Currently, this distinction is not taken into account in income-based poverty statistics. A household could have income from employment which puts it marginally over the 60 per cent of median income poverty line, yet at the same time be faced with large monthly rental payments. A retired couple could have a slightly lower income, just enough to put them below the poverty line, but may have no housing costs. The poverty statistics show the first household to be non-poor and the last household to be poor. Yet, when housing costs are considered, their relative positions may reverse.

Addressing this difficulty

The challenge, therefore, is to find a way to reflect the reality of housing expenditures and their differential impacts across society in the analysis of relative income poverty. Two possible approaches are examined below. The first is the housing expenditures approach and the second is the imputed rent approach.

Housing expenditures approach

The housing expenditures approach focuses on what people actually spend on accessing housing, either through rental payments or the purchase costs of home-ownership. Central to this approach is the reality that households, depending on their tenure arrangements, will spend widely varying amounts of income to obtain similar housing services which can in turn lead to them having differing shares of their income left over for other consumption needs. Accordingly, the housing expenditures approach aims to adjust household income in order to correct for these differences in the levels of housing expenditure across households.

The UK has adopted the housing expenditures approach in the production of its Households Below Average Income (HBAI) series. Here statistics are presented on two bases. The first is the before housing costs (BHC) basis, where statistics are derived from the analysis of disposable income in the conventional way. The second is the after housing costs (AHC) basis, derived by subtracting, from the disposable income of a household, a measure of housing costs in respect of the following items: rent; water rates, community water charges and council water charges; mortgage interest payments (net of tax relief); structural insurance premiums; and ground rent and service charges (DWP, 2005). The AHC poverty rate is obtained by recalculating the 60 per cent of median income poverty threshold after these deductions are made and seeing which households now have incomes below the new threshold.

The BHC/AHC distinction is made principally to take into account variations in housing costs that themselves do not correspond to comparable variations in the quality of housing. This is because any income measure that does not deduct housing costs may overstate the living standards of individuals whose housing costs are high relative to the quality of their accommodation. The converse also applies where the relative living standards could be understated for those individuals who were actually benefiting from a better quality of housing by paying more for their accommodation. Fahey *et al.* (2004b) suggest that the AHC income measure, by focusing on the income available for non-housing consumption, is more comparable across households than the conventional BHC measure.

Using data from the 2000 LIIS, Fahey *et al.* set out to apply the UK approach to assess the impact of housing expenditures on the extent and complexion of poverty and social inequalities in Ireland. Table 7.3 summarises their findings in respect of the impact of housing costs on poverty rates for the main tenure categories.

The first notable observation is that the inclusion of housing expenditures in the analysis of relative income poverty has little impact on the overall poverty rate, reducing it by only 0.8 per cent. This could be explained as follows: when housing costs are deducted from disposable household incomes across the income distribution, the disposable household income of the median household will also fall. Consequently the poverty threshold calculated as 60 per cent of median income will be lower than before. However, the amount by which median household income and the poverty threshold fall is limited by the fact that in 1999/2000, some 47 per cent of all dwellings in the state were owned outright and consequently would not incur rental or mortgage costs. The fall in the poverty threshold will cause some people with little or no housing expenditures and whose household incomes were just below the old threshold to rise above the new threshold leading to a fall in the poverty rate. The fall in the poverty rate, however, may be offset by other households with significant housing costs now falling below the threshold when their housing costs are deducted from their household income.

More significant changes between the BHC and AHC bases are observed at the level of particular tenure categories. For instance, when housing costs are taken into account, more owners of private and former local authority houses with mortgages find themselves in poverty, reflecting the burden of these mortgage costs. Also, as one might expect, far fewer outright owners of private or former local authority housing find themselves in poverty when housing expenditures are incorporated into the analysis. There is a modest drop in the rate of poverty for those renting local authority housing, reflecting the fact that they have lower housing costs than households paying a mortgage or renting privately.

Table 7.3: *Poverty rates before and after housing costs by tenure, 2000*

| | % below 60 per cent of median income | | Difference |
	BHC	AHC	
Outright owner of private housing	24.3	19.7	−4.6
Owner of private housing with mortgage	11.4	13.0	+1.6
Outright owner of (former) local authority housing	27.8	21.4	−6.4
Owner of (former) local authority housing with mortgage	22.5	24.6	+2.1
Private renter	19.2	27.5	+8.3
Social/local authority renter	62.2	60.8	−1.4
All	22.1	21.3	−0.8

Source: Fahey *et al.* (2004a)

Table 7.3 clearly illustrates the dramatic rise in the proportion of private renters falling below the poverty threshold when their rental costs are taken into account. On a BHC basis the poverty rate for private renters was 19.2 per cent. When rent expenditures are taken into account that figure is almost 50 per cent higher at 27.5 per cent. This provides further evidence of the increasing burden of housing costs being felt by those in the private rented sector and highlights them as a group that is increasingly vulnerable and at risk of poverty.

Looking at the breakdown of poverty rates according to the labour force status of the household reference person, Fahey *et al.* observe that there is remarkably little difference between the poverty rates recorded before housing costs are factored into the analysis and after. Table 7.4 shows that only the retired record a significant change, with their poverty rate falling from 33.8 per cent on a BHC basis to 26.9 per cent on an AHC basis. This outcome is to be expected because the AHC basis takes into account the fact that the vast majority of those in retirement do not have rental or mortgage costs. Poverty rates for employees and the self-employed rise marginally when housing costs are taken into account, perhaps reflecting the burden of mortgage or rental payments for some members of these groups.

Table 7.4: *Poverty rates before and after housing costs by labour force status, 2000*

| | % below 60 per cent of median income | | Difference |
	BHC	AHC	
Employee	7.4	8.4	+1.0
Self-employed	20.8	22.3	+1.5
Farmer	24.3	21.0	−3.3
Unemployed	50.7	53.7	+3.0
Ill/disabled	54.4	53.4	−1.0
Retired	33.8	26.9	−6.9
Home duties	47.6	44.3	−3.3
All	22.1	21.3	−0.8

Source: Fahey *et al.* (2004a)

Fahey *et al.* analyse the profile of those who fall below the poverty line when housing expenditures are taken into account and find that they are predominantly young, with 71 per cent in households where the reference person is under 35 years and only 2 per cent in households where the reference person is aged 65 and over. In terms of labour force status, they are predominantly in the workforce rather than retired. About one-third are in rented accommodation, a figure which is well above the national average of 11 per cent in 2002. The remaining two-thirds are owner-occupiers with mortgage costs. This provides further evidence of the burden of housing costs faced by those in the early stages of family formation.

In a further study, Fahey *et al.* (2004b) show, using data from the 1996 ECHP survey, that Ireland is unique in European terms as the only country which recorded a lower rate of relative income poverty on an AHC basis than on the usual BHC basis. Table 7.5 shows that the poverty rates in twelve of the other member states analysed rose, in some cases quite significantly, after an adjustment for housing expenditures was made.

Table 7.5: *Poverty rates before and after housing costs for fourteen EU member states, 1996*

| | % below 60 per cent of median income | | Difference |
	BHC	AHC	
Austria	16	19	+3
Belgium	16	18	+2
Denmark	11	18	+7
Finland	10	14	+4
France	17	20	+3
Germany	15	18	+3
Greece	21	23	+2
Ireland	**22**	**20**	**–2**
Italy	18	20	+2
Luxembourg	13	16.5	+3.5
Netherlands	14	20	+6
Portugal	24	24	0
Spain	18	19	+1
UK	19	24	+5

Source: Fahey *et al.* (2004b)

Fahey *et al.* (2004b) highlight a number of issues in relation to the housing expenditures approach. The first relates to the treatment of mortgage costs. They suggest that, on a strict interpretation, only the interest element of mortgage costs should be treated as being equivalent to rent, since the repayment of the principal borrowed relates to the acquisition of an asset rather than a payment for housing services. Therefore, total mortgage expenditures cannot be regarded as housing costs which are equivalent to rents. However, a looser interpretation suggests that, where the focus is with establishing the income remaining for non-housing-related consumption, then rent and mortgage payments (including the portion of the payment going towards the principal) should be treated as more or less equivalent housing-related drains on income to be corrected for in the same way.

A second issue with the housing expenditures approach is that it has limited capacity to take account of consumer choice and affordability factors. For example, certain households may elect to spend more on their housing needs than others, either by paying more in rent or by taking out a larger mortgage, in order to obtain a higher standard of housing. Other households may have their choices constrained by their income so that they cannot spend the required amount on housing to obtain a dwelling suited to their needs.

A final issue relates to the re-mortgaging of owner-occupied housing for general consumption purposes, where the net effect is to extract equity from the housing stock. It would be misleading to include such mortgage costs as expenditures on housing.

Fahey *et al.* conclude that, in light of these issues, the AHC measure represents a different but not necessarily a better account of a household's command over resources than the conventional BHC measure. Reflecting the reality that neither measure probably gives the full picture and that the truth may lie somewhere in between, the UK continues to publish figures on both bases.

Imputed rent approach
The second approach to incorporating housing into the analysis of poverty is to regard housing costs saved as a benefit or source of 'hidden income' to be valued and included in household income. Whereas the housing expenditures approach dealt with what people actually spend to access housing, the imputed rent approach focuses on notional income from housing. Hidden income arising from owner-occupied housing can be defined as the imputed rent which owner-occupiers, as tenants, would notionally pay themselves as occupiers (or alternatively the expenditure they save by not renting similar properties) (CSO, 2003). The figures used for this rent are the market rents for comparable housing in the private rented sector (Fahey *et al.*, 2004b). The imputed rent approach therefore represents an attempt to capture the real differences in living standards between a household paying rent and another in owner-occupied housing with no debt outstanding.

Atkinson *et al.* (2005) argue that failure to take this hidden income into account can give a misleading impression as to the relative situation of certain population sub-groups, for example older people who own their homes versus young families or single adults who are frequently either renting or in the early stages of house purchase. This distortion has been highlighted in the analysis above.

In a paper presented to its meeting in November 1998, Eurostat's Statistical Programme Committee proposed that imputed rent could be considered a relevant component of disposable income for two reasons. First, it represents a relatively high proportion in relation to total income. Second, its distribution within member states makes this component differ between household types. Using 1994 Household Budget Survey data from selected EU countries, the committee's task force set out to analyse the impact on relative income poverty rates of including imputed rent in the definition of income.

Table 7.6 summarises the results for a selection of EU member states. It shows the poverty rate, based on 60 per cent of median income, firstly using the conventional definition of income and secondly when imputed rent is included. The inclusion of imputed rent changes the percentages of poor persons, with the rate of poverty falling in five out of the seven member states analysed. The task force observes that this is particularly true for certain sub-populations such as the elderly. This finding prompted the committee to conclude that imputed rent plays a significant role in establishing income poverty thresholds and, therefore, the rates of poverty and ranking of countries after this component is included. It recommended the inclusion of imputed rent in the ECHP survey as a means of producing a more complete picture of the distribution of income (Eurostat, 1998).

Table 7.6: *Relevance to recorded poverty rates of the inclusion of imputed rent in the income definition, 1994*

| | % below 60 per cent of median income | | Difference |
	ECHP definition (%)	With imputed rent (%)	
Belgium	15.3	13.7	−1.6
Denmark	16.6	16.8	+0.2
Greece	21.1	19.3	−1.8
Spain	15.8	13.7	−2.1
Netherlands	15.8	16.3	+0.5
Portugal	20.1	19.4	−0.7
Finland	14.7	14.2	−0.5

Source: Eurostat (1998)

Frick and Grabka (2002) set out to investigate whether or not the income advantages derived from owner-occupied housing, as reflected by employing the imputed rent approach, exacerbate or level out existing differences in income in the UK, Germany (West) and the US in the 1990s. Table 7.7 shows that in all three countries owner-occupiers enjoyed a higher income position relative to the population average before imputed rent was included. When imputed rent was included in the analysis, this position further improved by several percentage points.

Looking at the breakdown between those who own their homes outright and those who have a mortgage, Frick and Grabka observe that the relative income position of outright owners before imputed rent is factored in is much lower than that of mortgage-holders, and in the case of the US their relative position is lower than the average for the total population. The higher income position of owners with a mortgage relates to the lifecycle, in that these persons are usually integrated into the labour market whereas the majority of outright owners tend to live on old-age pensions. However, the inclusion of imputed rent acts to significantly increase the relative income position of those who own their homes outright, reflecting the 'benefit' or 'hidden income' derived from outright ownership. It has the opposite effect on those with mortgages: slightly reducing their relative income position in all three countries.

The position of renters was found to be in stark contrast to that of home-owners. In all three countries the relative position of renters was below the average for the total population. The inclusion of imputed rent, which benefits outright homeowners and those paying below market rents, therefore results in a further deterioration in the relative position of renters.

Table 7.7: *The impact of imputed rent (IR) in the UK, West Germany and the US, 1997/1998*

	UK (1998)		West Germany (1998)		US (1997)	
	Before IR	*IR included*	*Before IR*	*IR included*	*Before IR*	*IR included*
	Relative income position: Total population = 100					
Total	100	100	100	100	100	100
All owner-occupiers	111	113	113	117	112	115
Owned outright	102	116	106	116	78	87
With mortgage	114	112	119	118	128	127
Renters	70	62	89	85	72	67

Source: Frick and Grabka (2002)

Frick and Grabka find, *inter alia*, that the inclusion of imputed rent results in a decrease in income inequality in Germany (West) and the US, while the UK recorded a small increase in overall income inequality. They also find that the inclusion of imputed rent yields a particular improvement in the measured wellbeing of the elderly in all three countries.

There are a number of conceptual and methodological difficulties with the imputed rent approach which have so far prevented its introduction at EU level. However, it is envisaged that the value of imputed rent will eventually be estimated and included in household income (Atkinson *et al.*, 2005). To facilitate this, data has been collected in response to the following question as part of the EU-SILC survey since its introduction in

Ireland in 2003: How much do you think you would pay as monthly rent (net of charges for heating, electricity etc.) if you rented a similar unfurnished dwelling?

The imputed rent approach is similar to the approach taken in calculating the national accounts, where rents are imputed to arrive at estimates of hidden income from housing at an aggregated level. In poverty measurement, where the household is the unit of analysis, imputed rents would be required at the household level, based on the market value of housing owned by different household categories. However, the difficulty is that this data is not readily available so that imputation can end up being based on assumptions that do not necessarily accord with reality.

There is the potential for inaccuracies to arise in response to the EU-SILC question above. For example, Frick and Grabka suggest that the possibility of over-estimation of imputed rents can arise where owner-occupiers are asked directly to estimate the amount of rent that they would have to pay if they lived in their home as tenants. Inaccuracies can also arise where respondents may not have the necessary information about the market value of similar houses in the area, leading them to resort to guessing an appropriate figure. One could find, therefore, that the imputed rents derived by this subjective method may not accord with actual market values.

Furthermore, while it can be argued that the exclusion of imputed rent can give a misleading impression, similar concerns arise in relation to its inclusion. As Atkinson *et al.* (2005) point out, the rent imputed to a household is not in fact equivalent to cash income received in the conventional sense as it cannot be used to meet other expenditure needs. Focusing solely on income including imputed rent has important implications from a social inclusion perspective. This is because a misleading impression of a household's capacity to avoid poverty and deprivation could be given, where a significant figure for imputed rent is included in that household's income. For example, an elderly woman who owns a large house outright may not be faced with housing-related expenditure but the substantial rent that would be imputed because of the size of the house is not available to pay for food, clothing and heating costs. This must be balanced against the fact that she does clearly enjoy some benefit from owning her own house and is better placed than her neighbour who is a tenant.

One of the main disadvantages of the imputed rent approach is that it is a notional concept, as compared to the housing expenditures approach which focuses on what people actually spend on accessing housing. Also imputed rent is very difficult to estimate in Ireland because of the relatively small private rental market and the differences between rented and owner-occupied housing (CSO, 2003).

Due to these conceptual and methodological concerns, Atkinson *et al.* recommend that, while poverty indicators inclusive of imputed rent will be of value in terms of obtaining a more comprehensive picture, it will be important, in the interests of a balanced analysis, to continue to produce such indicators exclusive of imputed rent.

Conclusions and implications

Currently, housing considerations are not included in the analysis of income and the measurement of poverty in Ireland. Yet such considerations are clearly significant in the Irish context. Average house prices in Ireland increased by 241 per cent between 1996 and 2005. The position of mortgage holders deteriorated markedly, with mortgage costs rising from €28.71 per week (in 2000 terms) in 1973 to €73.19 per week in 2000. The situation in the private rental sector is particularly worrying with rents soaring by 259 per cent in real terms between 1973 and 2000, in sharp contrast to the relatively stable costs of accommodation rented from local authorities.

The preceding analysis showed that in 1999/2000 almost half of all dwellings (47 per cent) in the state were owned outright. The data showed that these owner-occupiers with no mortgage costs are heavily concentrated in the older population age groups. Fahey *et al.* (2004a) note that, at a given level of income, a household which must spend 25 per cent of its income on rent or mortgage payments is in a very different position to the outright owner with no such payments.

In order to address this difficulty, this chapter firstly examined the housing expenditures approach, as used in the UK, which aims to adjust household income in order to correct for differences in the levels of housing expenditures across households. Applied in an Irish context, it leads only to a marginal (0.8 per cent) fall in the overall relative income poverty rate, due to offsetting effects. At the disaggregated level, poverty rates fall for outright owners and social renters, the retired and farmers, but rise for private renters, mortgage-holders, the unemployed, the employed and the self-employed.

The housing expenditures approach, however, is not without its problems, prompting the conclusion that it provides a different but not necessarily a better account of a household's command over resources and that, were such an approach to be adopted in Ireland, it would be prudent to present figures for before and after housing costs on the grounds that the truth probably lies somewhere in between.

Although the analysis did not show housing expenditures having a major adverse impact on owner-occupiers with mortgages overall, it did highlight the particularly vulnerable position of young adults and those in the early stages of family formation. Therefore, there may be a case for further research to focus on the impact of housing costs specifically on those who took out mortgages in the last five years, for example, as the effect on these groups may be obscured by figures averaged across all those with mortgages, including those who took out mortgages fifteen or twenty years ago and whose payments would be small by current standards.

A second approach to addressing this problem is known as the imputed rent approach. In contrast to the housing expenditures approach, the imputed rent approach is concerned with the benefit of housing costs saved by people who own their homes outright or who are paying subsidised rents. As with the housing expenditures approach, the inclusion of imputed rent improves the relative position of outright homeowners. This finding has significant implications for Ireland where nearly half of all dwellings are owned outright.

It also has implications for the position of the retired as presented in poverty statistics. In Chapter 3 we noted that 27.1 per cent of those aged over 65 were living below the 60 per cent of median income poverty line. Given that over 80 per cent of those aged 65 to 74 own their own home outright, the incorporation of imputed rent could significantly improve the relative position of, and reduce poverty rates for, the retired population sub-group in Ireland.

The analysis highlighted the fact that while the housing expenditures approach and the imputed rent approach are effective ways of dealing with the housing issue in the measurement and analysis of poverty, they are not without their problems, criticisms and shortcomings. It is recommended that these issues need to be considered more fully in the context of any evaluation or assessment of their utility and applicability in an Irish context.

Finally, it must be noted that there are other possibilities for incorporating housing into the analysis of poverty and social exclusion which may merit further investigation. For example, Atkinson et al. (2005) recommend that further thought should be given to devising a measure which would identify those seriously at risk of poverty/exclusion due to housing costs. Here the focus would be on the 'uncompensated burden' of housing costs faced by those on low incomes. It would involve subtracting housing-related cash transfers from total household income, and calculating the proportion that the 'uncovered' housing costs (i.e. expenditure on housing less support received to cover it) comprise of that income. Atkinson *et al.* propose that those with income 'net of housing support' falling below some income threshold and whose uncovered housing costs comprise more than a certain proportion of income (net of housing assistance) could be identified as seriously at risk of poverty/exclusion due to housing costs – with the appropriate income threshold and critical proportion themselves the subject of analysis. A possible obstacle to this approach for some EU countries is that housing-related cash transfers are not always distinguished from other forms of social transfer.

8

Scope for Criticism of the Consistent Poverty Measure

Difficulty stated

Conflicting trends which emerged as a result of the change from the LIIS to the EU-SILC have impacted on the credibility of Ireland's consistent poverty measure. At the same time, questions have also been asked as to whether the measure continues to give an adequate reflection of what it means to be poor in Ireland in the twenty-first century.

Difficulty explained and justified

The consistent poverty measure was developed by the ESRI using the results of the 1987 Survey of Poverty, Income Distribution and Use of State Services. The measure was an attempt to employ the double criterion of income and deprivation in consumption to produce a measure that would identify the sector of the population experiencing generalised deprivation or exclusion due to lack of resources. The ESRI employed a statistical technique known as factor analysis on data from the 1987 survey to select a list of basic necessities which would best serve, together with income, as indicators of generalised deprivation. From this process, the eight basic deprivation items (see Table 8.2) were identified as a cluster of items that 'every household should be able to have and that nobody should have to do without' (Nolan, 2002).

People are considered to be in 'consistent poverty' if they have an income below the relative income poverty threshold (in other words, an equivalised disposable income less than 60 per cent of the median) and are living in a household deprived of one or more of the eight basic deprivation items. In the 1997 National Anti-Poverty Strategy (NAPS), a global poverty reduction target was framed around this measure.

A criticism of the consistent poverty measure, particularly since the late 1990s, is that it no longer adequately reflects the nature of poverty in contemporary Ireland. The report of the Benchmarking and Indexation Group (2001) notes that critics of the measure suggest it fails to capture the reality of living in poverty because it places too much emphasis on very basic living conditions. This results in an understatement of the true level of poverty. This criticism stems from the fact that the eight basic necessities that comprise the deprivation index component of the measure remained unchanged from 1987 to 2007.[2] In 2005, Nolan *et al.* pointed out that the items relating to two pairs of strong shoes or a warm waterproof overcoat could be regarded as more appropriate to an earlier more frugal era in Ireland.

Layte *et al.* (2000) highlight the practical implications of this situation in terms of the global poverty reduction target included in the 1997 NAPS. This target was framed around the data for consistent poverty for 1994, which was the most recent available (see Table 8.1). The NAPS contained a two-pronged target to reduce consistent poverty at the 60 per cent of mean income threshold from 15 per cent to below 10 per cent and, at the 50 per cent of mean income line, from 9 per cent to below 5 per cent. The 60 per cent of mean income consistent poverty target to be achieved by 2007 was actually met in 1997. While the fall in deprivation during the mid to late 1990s was a welcome development, it did, quite legitimately, prompt the question as to whether an unchanged set of indicators can continue to capture adequately what is regarded as generalised deprivation at a time of rising living standards.

Table 8.1: *Consistent poverty rates based on mean income lines, 1987–1997*

	1987	*1994*	*1997*
50% of mean income	9.8	9.0	7.3
60% of mean income	16.0	15.0	9.9

Source: Layte *et al.* (2000)

Layte *et al.* (2001a) explain that the conceptual underpinnings of the consistent poverty measure do not, as might be suggested, encourage an absolutist notion of poverty to be measured against a fixed standard, but in fact highlight the need to revise and adapt the non-monetary deprivation indicators to take account of improved living standards and changing views about what are the basic necessities. They propose that, where there is significant change in either living standards or views about necessities, the need to revise the deprivation component of the consistent poverty

---

[2] Since this analysis was conducted the ESRI has published proposals to revise the consistent poverty measure. However, as the central concern of this analysis is an ongoing issue, it remains relevant to an overall consideration of poverty measurement problems.

measure may arise. Nolan (2002) reinforces this view on the part of the ESRI when he says, 'It must be emphasised that the combined poverty measure developed by my colleagues and myself was never intended to be a mixture of relative income and absolute or fixed deprivation indicators'.

Layte *et al.* (2001a) contend that the need to review the consistent poverty measure is reinforced by the fact that incomes and living standards in Ireland increased so dramatically during the 1990s, as illustrated in Figure 8.1. Against the backdrop of rapidly increasing income and improving living standards, deprivation levels fell quite considerably between 1994 and 2001, from over 25 per cent to little over 8 per cent, when measured using an unchanged set of deprivation indicators.

Figure 8.1: *Evolution of GNP per capita and the incidence of deprivation*, 1987–2001*

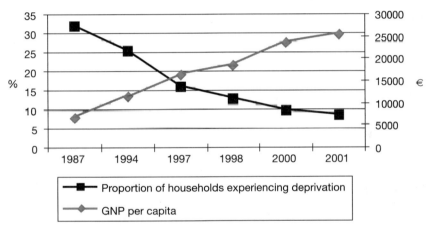

* A household is regarded to be experiencing deprivation if it is deprived of one or more of the eight basic deprivation items
Sources: CSO Database Direct, Layte *et al.* (2001a) and Callan *et al.* (1993)

Table 8.2 shows how the proportion of households/persons reporting deprivation of each of the eight deprivation indicators in the consistent poverty deprivation index changed between 1987 and 2004. Although the data for 1987 is based on households and the data for 2004 from the EU-SILC focuses on persons, the figures are still broadly comparable because evidence suggests that, in terms of deprivation at least, members of households tend to share the same standard of living (Layte *et al.*, 2000).

The table shows that deprivation levels for seven out of the eight items have fallen over the period. The only exception is the 'no substantial meal' indicator, which shows a slight increase. In many cases the falls are quite dramatic. For example, the proportion of those unable to afford a roast dinner once a week fell from 13 per cent in 1987 to 4.5 per cent in 2004, while the proportion of those unable to afford two pairs of strong shoes fell from 11 per cent in 1987 to 3.8 per cent in 2004.

Table 8.2: *Households/persons deprived of the basic deprivation items, 1987 and 2004*

	% deprived of selected item	
	1987 *(households)*	*2004* *(persons)*
No substantial meal on at least one day in the past two weeks	4.4	5.2
Without heating at some stage in the past year	6.5	5.4
Experienced debt problems arising from ordinary living expenses	14.2	8.7
Unable to afford two pairs of strong shoes	11.0	3.8
Unable to afford a roast once a week	13.0	4.5
Unable to afford a meal with meat, chicken or fish every second day	9.0	3.7
Unable to afford new, not second-hand, clothes	8.0	5.8
Unable to afford a warm waterproof coat	8.0	2.7

Sources: Whelan *et al.* (1991) and CSO (2005b)

Focusing on the twenty deprivation items for which information is available, Table 8.3 highlights how views on what constitutes necessities changed from 1987 to 1997. In general, a greater proportion of people regarded each item as a necessity in 1997 than did in 1987. For example, in 1987, three items – a daily newspaper, a telephone and a colour television – were not regarded as necessities by a majority. By 1997, only the daily newspaper failed to command majority support, with the proportion regarding it as a necessity dropping from 40 per cent in 1987 to 33 per cent. There were particularly large increases in the proportion of households regarding a telephone, colour television, car, central heating and a week's annual holiday away from home as necessities.

Table 8.3 provides further evidence of the increase in living standards between 1987 and 1998 with a significant reduction in the numbers lacking items and in the extent of enforced deprivation. In particular, the proportion of households lacking each of the five items on the basic list for which information is available had reached very low levels. There were also striking falls in the proportion of households experiencing enforced lack of certain secondary items including a car, the ability to save some of one's income regularly, a week's holiday away from home, central heating

Table 8.3: *Households that consider deprivation items to be a necessity and those suffering enforced lack of each item, 1987 and 1997/1998*

	% stating as a necessity*		% suffering enforced lack	
	1987	1997	1987	1998
Primary deprivation				
Whether there was a day during the previous two weeks when the household manager did not have a substantial meal	N/A	N/A		
Whether the household manager had to go without heating during the last year through lack of money	N/A	N/A		
Debt problems:	N/A	N/A		
• Household is currently in arrears on rent, mortgage, ESB and gas				
• Had to go into debt to meet ordinary living expenses				
• Had to sell or pawn anything worth £50 or more				
• Has received assistance from a private charity in the past year				
New, not second-hand, clothes	78	86	8	5
Meal with meat, chicken or fish	86	94	9	2
Two pairs of strong shoes	87	96	11	3
A warm waterproof coat	93	93	8	2
A roast meat joint or its equivalent once a week	68	76	13	3
Secondary deprivation				
A hobby or leisure activity	71	70	13	8
A daily newspaper	40	33	16	8
Telephone	47	82	31	8
Central heating	53	81	29	10
To be able to save some of one's income regularly	88	82	55	33
A week's annual holiday away from home (not with relatives)	50	62	49	29
Car	59	82	22	12
Head of household has not had an afternoon or evening out in the last fortnight that costs money, because of lack of resources	N/A	N/A		
Presents for friends or family once a year	63	73	13	5

Table 8.3: *Households that consider deprivation items to be a necessity and those suffering enforced lack of each item, 1987 and 1997/1998 (contd)*

	% stating as a necessity*		% suffering enforced lack	
	1987	1997	1987	1998
Housing and household capital deprivation				
Bath or shower	98	99	7	2
Indoor toilet	99	99	6	2
Washing machine	85	93	10	4
Refrigerator	94	99	2	1
Colour television	36	70	9	1
A dry damp-free dwelling	99	99	9	4
Heating for the living rooms when it is cold	99	99	3	4

* This question is asked for twenty of the twenty-four items; N/A = not asked
Sources: Layte *et al.* (2001a) and Whelan *et al.* (1991)

and a telephone. Enforced deprivation levels for the household items are negligible in most cases. Mindful of these trends, Nolan (2002) points out that the ESRI looked in depth at whether the set of items serving to capture generalised deprivation needs to be expanded or adapted so as to better reflect the current situation.

Addressing this difficulty

UK research provides a useful insight into the changing expectations associated with rising living standards and how they can be reflected in the way that deprivation is measured. Research examining changes between the Breadline Britain Surveys of 1983 and 1990 and the 1999 Poverty and Social Exclusion (PSE) survey concludes that over time a greater proportion of people came to regard items as necessities (Gordon and Pantazis, 1997; Gordon *et al.*, 2000c).

The 1990 Breadline Britain Survey, for example, developed and extended the methodology of the original 1983 study including a larger number of deprivation items (44 compared to 35 in 1983). The 1999 PSE survey further developed the process, increasing the number of items to 54 for adults aged over 16 and adding a further 30 items for children, reported on separately. In addition, three items included in 1983 and 1990 were omitted: an inside toilet not shared with another household, a bath not shared with another household and a pack of cigarettes every other day. The first two were dropped on the basis that virtually all households had inside toilet and bath facilities by the end of the 1990s. It was decided to omit the question relating to cigarettes because, as an addictive drug, cigarettes could not be considered to be a good indicator of poverty.

The UK studies, pioneered by Mack and Lansley, adopt what is known as the 'socially perceived necessities' approach to deprivation measurement. What this means is that once the initial list of deprivation items is compiled, a survey is then conducted to establish which items are regarded by a majority of the population to be necessities. Those items deemed a necessity by more than 50 per cent of respondents can, therefore, be considered as 'socially perceived necessities'. A follow-up survey is then conducted to establish what proportion of the population is deprived of these necessities.

In the UK, the Omnibus Survey undertaken by the Office for National Statistics in June 1999 included questions designed to establish from a sample of the general population what items and activities they considered necessities. The results from this survey informed the 1999 PSE survey which followed after and which set out to establish what proportion of the population was deprived of such necessities. The PSE survey also obtained a wealth of other information on poverty and social exclusion in Britain.

Overall, as Table 8.4 shows, the list of items which the British public was asked to rate as necessities or not grew over the period from 1983 to 1999. Many of the items added relate to social customs such as visiting friends or family, attending weddings or funerals, attending worship and so on. Inability to afford to undertake these activities could indicate that a person is socially excluded. Also, a range of contemporary material goods has been added in order to determine the extent to which these have come to be regarded as necessities. Some of these goods, such as a fridge freezer, were considered by a majority to be a necessity; many others, such as a home computer, were not considered necessities. However, as living standards continue to rise and tastes and norms in society evolve, some of these items may come to be regarded as necessities in future surveys.

Table 8.5 illustrates clearly what Gordon and Pantazis (1997) term 'the relative theory of poverty', which predicts that the number of people who perceive common possessions and activities as necessary will increase as a society becomes richer. This provides further evidence, in light of the significant rise in Irish living standards, of the need to revisit regularly the number and type of deprivation indicators in Irish surveys.

A number of items, however, were regarded as necessities by fewer people in 1999 than in earlier surveys. For example, the percentages for such items as carpets and two pairs of all-weather shoes have fallen. In the case of the new, not second-hand, clothes item, a majority (65 per cent) of people considered this a necessity in 1990 but by 1999 this had become a minority (48 per cent). Once again, the UK experience points to the need

Table 8.4: *Changing deprivation items and proportions deeming each item a necessity, UK, 1983–1999*

| | % stating as necessity | | |
	1999	1990	1983
A damp-free home	93	98	96
An inside toilet	~	97	96
Heating to warm	94	97	97
Beds for everyone	95	97	97
Bath not shared	~	95	94
A decent state of decoration	82	92	~
Fridge	89	92	77
Public transport for one's own needs	~	~	88
Warm waterproof coat	85	91	87
Three meals a day for kids	**91**	90	82
Two meals a day for adults	91	90	64
Insurance	79	88	~
Fresh fruit	86	88	~
Toys for kids	**84**	84	71
Separate bedrooms for children aged 10+	**80**	82	77
Carpets	67	78	70
Meat and fish every other day	79	77	63
Celebrations on special occasions	83	74	69
Two pairs of all-weather shoes	64	74	78
Self-contained accommodation	~	~	79
Washing machine	76	73	67
Presents for friends/family	56	69	63
Out-of-school activities	~	69	~
Regular savings	66	68	~
Hobby or leisure activity	78	67	64
New, not second-hand, clothes	48	65	64
A roast joint or equivalent	56	64	67
Leisure equipment	~	61	57
Garden	~	~	55
TV	56	58	51
Phone	71	56	43
Annual week's holiday	55	54	63
A best outfit	51	54	48
Outing for kids weekly	~	53	40
Children's friends round to play	**59**	52	37
A dressing gown	34	42	38
A night out fortnightly	37	42	36
Fares to visit friends	38	39	~
Special lessons	~	39	~
Friends or family round for a meal	64	37	32
Car	38	26	22
Pack of cigarettes	~	18	14

Table 8.4: *Changing deprivation items and proportions deeming each item a necessity, UK, 1983–1999 (contd)*

| | % stating as necessity | | |
	1999	1990	1983
A monthly meal in a restaurant/pub	26	17	~
Holidays abroad	19	17	~
Video	19	13	~
Home computer	11	5	~
Dishwasher	7	4	~
Dictionary	53	~	~
Replace broken electrical goods	85	~	~
Visits to friends/family	84	~	~
Visiting friends/family in hospital	92	~	~
Replace worn-out old furniture	54	~	~
Microwave	23	~	~
Mobile phone	7	~	~
Tumble drier	20	~	~
Satellite TV	5	~	~
CD player	12	~	~
Deep freeze/fridge freezer	68	~	~
Appropriate clothes	69	~	~
Medicines prescribed by doctor	90	~	~
Access to the Internet	6	~	~
Money for self	59	~	~
Daily newspaper	30	~	~
Visit to the pub fortnightly	20	~	~
Attend weddings/funerals	80	~	~
Attending place of worship	42	~	~
Collect children from school	75	~	~
Visits to school (e.g. sports day)	81	~	~
No. of items considered necessities	35 (+ 4 children's items)	32	26
No. of items not considered necessities	19	12	9
Total no. of items	54 +4*	44	35

~ data was not collected
* 54 adult items; 4 children's items are included here for comparison with previous studies – these are highlighted in bold
Sources: Gordon *et al.* (2000c) and Mack and Lansley (1985)

to review and update the list of deprivation indicators underlying any measure of deprivation regularly.

Finally, Table 8.4 shows the number of items endorsed by the public as socially perceived necessities which formed the basis of subsequent analysis into the experience of poverty and deprivation in Britain. In 1983, research was based on twenty-six socially perceived necessities, rising to thirty-two in 1990 and thirty-five in 1999. Gordon *et al.* (2000c) explain that the new questions added to the 1999 survey were derived from a combination of sources including discussions amongst the research team, focus group analysis, the ECHP Survey Harmonised Question Set (consumer durables), Small Fortunes: National Survey of the Lifestyles and Living Standards of Children, the Swedish Living Standards Survey and the Lorraine Panel Survey.

Conclusions and implications

Irish society and living standards have changed considerably since 1987 when the consistent poverty measure was first devised and the deprivation questions forming the basis of the consistent poverty measure were selected. Yet the same set of deprivation items was in use over the following twenty years. This left the measure open to criticism that it no longer adequately reflects what it means to be poor in contemporary Ireland. It was argued that many of the deprivation items related to a more frugal era which suggested that a 1987 concept of poverty was being measured. This prompts questions as to the extent to which it can continue to be meaningful from a policy-making perspective. As living standards rise, is it possible for an unchanged set of indicators to continue to capture adequately what is regarded as generalised deprivation?

Calandrino (2003) argues that using the same basket of deprivation items year on year gives an absolute measure which produces results that may not gain public credibility. He attempted to replicate the 'consistent poverty' approach to British data for 1999 and 2001 using the same factor analysis technique used by the ESRI to construct the basic deprivation index. His findings show that the dimensions of deprivation varied across the two years. This, he suggests, confirms that factor analysis does not necessarily produce consistent results across different samples or over time. For Calandrino, the 'consistent poverty' approach yielded a significant decrease in those defined as both income-poor and deprived between 1999 and 2001.

Significantly, the ESRI points out that the consistent poverty measure was never intended to become an 'absolute' measure of poverty. Yet the evidence clearly shows that as Ireland prospered in the 1990s the proportion of the population experiencing enforced lack of each deprivation item dropped sharply. At the same time, for most items, the proportion of the population considering each as a necessity rose, reflecting the rising expectations of an increasingly prosperous country.

This evidence prompted the ESRI to conclude that the deprivation component of the consistent poverty measure needs to be updated in light of changing living standards and it has published proposals in this regard (Maître *et al.*, 2006).

In addressing this difficulty, the approach taken in the UK is instructive. Following an initial 1983 study, two successive studies (1990 and 1999) revisited the list of deprivation items used, taking out redundant items and adding new items. A survey was then undertaken using the new list to establish those items which a majority of the population regarded as necessities. The number of items included increased from thirty-five in the 1983 survey to forty-four in 1990 and fifty-four in 1999. Many of the added items reflected the increasing importance of social customs to people's quality of life and wellbeing.

In conclusion, therefore, the evolution in the lists of deprivation items in the UK highlights the changing nature of deprivation over time. It demonstrates the need to revisit regularly the way we measure deprivation and to update deprivation questions in light of changes in living standards and societal expectations. The UK studies are illuminating in so far as they demonstrate how this might be done. A rebasing of the consistent poverty measure using an updated list of deprivation items at regular intervals, perhaps every five years in line with the rebasing of the Consumer Price Index, would help to maximise the validity and relevance of the measure in the eyes of the public. Significantly, it would also ensure that consistent poverty continues to be a meaningful source of evidence-based information for the policy-maker.

9

Public Confusion

Difficulty stated

The way that poverty is currently measured and communicated often obscures clarity and frustrates society's understanding of how many people are poor in Ireland and who those people are. This difficulty poses significant challenges for the government, non-governmental organisations and others involved in communicating and using poverty statistics.

Difficulty explained and justified

There are several contributors to the confusion surrounding the level of poverty in Ireland. These include differences between the two key measures used – consistent poverty and relative income poverty; the damaging impact of significant data revisions; and the provision of multiple figures for a given indicator through the use of different methodologies to calculate poverty figures.

Relative income poverty versus consistent poverty

Figure 9.1 shows how the two most commonly used indicators of poverty in Ireland evolved over the period from 1994 to 2001. For reasons explored in Chapter 4, relative income poverty (calculated as the proportion of the population falling below a threshold of 60 per cent of median income) was comparatively high at just over 15 per cent in 1994. The rate of consistent poverty, in contrast, was just over 8 per cent in 1994. The fact that the rate of relative income poverty was higher than the rate of consistent poverty should not come as a surprise given that the consistently poor, by definition, are a subset of those in relative income poverty. However, the striking feature highlighted by Figure 9.1 is the diverging trend in the two poverty rates over the period. The relative income poverty rate rose continuously to just below 22 per cent in 2001. In sharp contrast, the rate of consistent poverty halved to just over 4 per cent in 2001. These conflicting trends contribute to the level of confusion among the general public in relation to the numbers in poverty in Ireland and the way in which poverty levels are changing over time.

Figure 9.1: *Relative income poverty* and consistent poverty, 1994–2001*

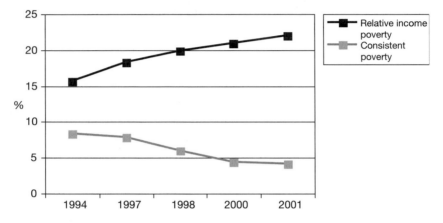

* Defined as 60 per cent of median income
Source: Whelan *et al.* (2003)

As well as showing conflicting trends in the overall level of poverty, the two key poverty indicators also paint conflicting pictures of the profile of those in poverty. This not only adds to public confusion but also has significant implications from a policy-making perspective. In an evidence-based policy-making environment, those responsible for formulating economic and social policy and targeting state resources require sound data in relation to who the poor in our society are and where they are located geographically. At present, as Table 9.1 shows, different conclusions are reached depending on which measure is used.

The relative income poverty measure suggests that poverty is most prevalent among those aged 65 and over, whereas the consistent poverty measure points to children as the lifecycle group most at risk of poverty. Looking at household composition, the relative income poverty measure suggests that households with two adults and no children face an above-average risk of poverty at 21.4 per cent compared to the rate for the total population of 19.4 per cent. The consistent poverty measure, however, shows that 4.7 per cent of people in this category are poor, which is well below the average rate for the population as a whole of 6.8 per cent.

Under principal economic status, the unemployed and the ill/disabled are the two groups with the highest rates of poverty under both measures. However, the relative income poverty measure suggests that the retired and

Table 9.1: *Relative income poverty* and consistent poverty, 2004*

	% of population in relative income poverty	*% of population in consistent poverty*
Total	19.4	6.8
Age group		
0–14	21.2	9.5
15–64	17.6	6.5
65+	27.1	3.3
Household composition		
1 adult, no children	35.7	9.9
2 adults, no children	21.4	4.7
3 or more adults, no children	12.7	3.5
1 adult with children	48.3	31.1
2 adults with 1 to 3 children	12.5	4.7
Other households with children	23.1	9.6
Location		
Urban areas	16.6	7.6
Rural areas	24.1	5.5
Principal economic status		
At work	7.0	1.8
Unemployed	37.2	19.2
Student	23.6	8.7
Home duties	32.1	9.6
Retired	26.1	3.7
Ill/disabled	47.3	21.7
Children (under 16)	21.9	9.9
Other	52.3	~

* Defined as 60 per cent of median income
~ Sample occurrence too small for estimation
Source: CSO (2005b)

those on home duties also face very high poverty levels, whereas under the consistent poverty measure both of these groups are shown to have proportionately much lower levels of poverty. Finally, the two measures produce conflicting information in relation to the geographic distribution of poverty. The relative income poverty measure suggests that poverty is more prevalent in rural areas, whereas the consistent poverty measure tells us that a higher proportion of those living in urban areas are poor than of those living in rural areas.

Data revisions
Although not an uncommon occurrence in the statistical sphere, the revision of published poverty statistics is highlighted here as a further issue

which challenges the task of clearly communicating poverty-related facts to the general public. Revisions also, it is argued, undermine the credibility of the measures by damaging the public's confidence in them (as well as the confidence of interest groups and policy-makers).

The first results from the EU-SILC in relation to 2003 were published by the CSO in January 2005. The 2003 data was subsequently revised to take account of improved re-weighting and calibration methods and a revised set of figures was published alongside the results for 2004 in December 2005.

The revisions to the 2003 data, although necessary, were quite significant. Table 9.2 shows the impact of the revisions on rates of relative income poverty and consistent poverty, which were both revised downwards. It also shows the impact on a number of the other Laeken social indicators including two measures of income inequality – the Gini coefficient and the quintile share ratio – and the poverty gap measure.

The most significant aspect of the 2003 revisions is the impact they had on overall trends. The initial 2003 data showed a continuation in the rising trend of relative income poverty from 21.9 per cent in 2001 to 22.7 per cent in 2003. It also showed falls in the Gini coefficient (30.3 per cent to 29.6 per cent) and the poverty gap (20.7 per cent to 16.3 per cent). The revision of the 2003 data presented a very different picture. The rising trend of relative income poverty was halted and the rate for 2003 (19.7 per cent) was now lower than the rate in 2001. The poverty gap, rather than falling significantly as initially reported, rose above the 2001 figure. Similarly, the Gini coefficient was shown to be rising instead of declining and the quintile share ratio, which had been more or less unchanged, rose from 4.8 in 2001 to 5.0.

While even minor revisions can create difficulties, the more fundamental changes between the initial and revised 2003 EU-SILC data have significant implications. This is because as well as reporting significant changes to key indicators, they revealed different trends.

At the disaggregated level, the revisions to the 2003 data led to a fall in the level of relative income poverty for all population sub-groups with the exception of lone parents. Initially it was reported that 42.3 per cent of lone parents were below the 60 per cent of median income threshold. The revised figures show that 48.3 per cent of lone parents were in poverty in 2003. Similarly, although the overall rate of consistent poverty was revised downward from 9.4 per cent to 8.8 per cent, the rates of consistent poverty for a number of the population sub-groups were revised upward. For example, initially it was reported that 26.4 per cent of the unemployed and

Table 9.2: *Impact of revisions to 2003 EU-SILC data on selected indicators*

	2000	2001	Initial	2003 Revised	Change
Relative income poverty* (%)	20.9	21.9	22.7	19.7	−3.0
Consistent poverty (%)	4.3	4.1	9.4	8.8	−0.6
Gini coefficient	30.2	30.3	29.6	31.1	+1.5
Income distribution (quintile share ratio)	4.7	4.8	4.7	5.0	+0.3
Poverty gap** (%)	19.3	20.7	16.3	21.5	+5.2

* Defined as 60 per cent of median income
** Defined as the difference between median income of persons below the poverty threshold and the poverty threshold, expressed as a percentage of the threshold
Source: CSO (2005b)

20.9 per cent of the ill/disabled were consistently poor, but these figures were later revised upwards to 28.3 per cent and 22.4 per cent respectively.

Use of different figures for the same indicator
Another key factor contributing to confusion and undermining public confidence in the system used to measure poverty arises when different figures are used and quoted for the same indicator. There are two reasons why this may happen.

The first stems from the selective use by bodies or organisations of those figures that best support their case. For example, a person or organisation wishing to highlight the seriousness of poverty in Ireland may focus on the relative income poverty measure as opposed to the consistent poverty measure, given that the rate of the former tends to be much higher than that of the latter. Within the relative income poverty measure they can choose to quote the domestic relative income poverty rate or the rate which is used by the EU for Ireland and which is calculated somewhat differently. As noted earlier, the rate of relative income poverty was 19.7 per cent in 2003 falling slightly to 19.4 per cent in 2004. However, a person or organisation wishing to suggest that poverty is a serious problem and becoming more prevalent may choose to focus instead on the EU-defined relative income poverty figures which were somewhat higher at 20.1 per cent in 2003 and rose rather than fell in 2004 to 20.9 per cent. Alternatively, they could opt to quote figures for poverty using a higher poverty threshold, say 70 per cent of median income.

Someone wishing to play down the level of poverty could focus instead on the consistent poverty measure, which shows poverty rates of 8.8 per cent in 2003 and 6.8 per cent in 2004. Consistent poverty was reported as low as 4.1 per cent in 2001 under the ESRI's LIIS. Alternatively, using the relative income measure, a lower poverty threshold could be selected, say 40 per cent of median income.

The existence of more than one measure of poverty, multiple derivatives of each measure and different versions of indicators (EU versus domestic) provides the scope for such manipulation. It is easy to appreciate how the general public might become confused and disengaged when faced with opposing sets of convincingly argued figures. Equally, it must be acknowledged that confusion and misunderstanding about the way poverty is measured can also give rise to the unintended misuse or misquoting of poverty statistics.

The second reason why different figures are quoted for a given indicator stems from the fact that there are different ways of calculating an indicator and its component parts. In the case of relative income poverty, for example, a range of factors influence the poverty rate obtained, including whether mean income or median income is used, which equivalence scale is used, whether the focus is on the household or the individual and the way that income is collected, measured and defined.

Mean versus median

Relative income poverty rates are calculated in terms of the percentage of the population falling below income thresholds derived as fixed proportions of mean or median income (see Chapter 2). The threshold of 60 per cent of median income was proposed by Eurostat in 1998 and is now widely used throughout Europe. Prior to this, however, average or mean income was commonly used and such figures still appear in many of the reports, studies and commentaries produced today.

The key point is that both methods – mean income and median income – will produce quite different figures for relative income poverty. This is because average income differs from median income. For example, in 2004 mean equivalised disposable household income was €18,773, whereas median equivalised disposable household income was €16,133. Table 9.3 shows the impact on 2001 poverty rates of using the mean or the median. As the median is generally lower than the mean (due to the skewed nature of the income distribution which is reflected in the mean), higher percentage thresholds are used for the median than for the mean, which is itself, it could be argued, a further confounding factor.

Table 9.3: *Poverty rates based on mean or median income, 2001*

	Relative income poverty (%)	Consistent poverty (%)
Mean		
Proportion under 40% threshold	8.1	2.5
Proportion under 50% threshold	18.4	4.1
Proportion under 60% threshold	27.5	5.2
Median		
Proportion under 50% threshold	12.9	2.9
Proportion under 60% threshold	21.9	4.1
Proportion under 70% threshold	29.3	4.9

Source: Whelan *et al.* (2003)

Table 9.3 highlights the dangers of confusing mean-based figures with median-based figures. For example, relative income poverty using a 60 per cent of mean income threshold was 27.5 per cent in 2001 compared to 21.9 per cent using the 60 per cent of median income threshold. Similarly, using a 60 per cent of mean income threshold with the consistent poverty measure would yield a poverty rate of 5.2 per cent instead of 4.1 per cent based on the median. The challenge in reviewing trends in the data over time is that median-based data prevails from 2001 onwards, whereas most of the data for the 1990s and before is based on the mean.

Multiple equivalence scales
Table 9.4 shows the rates of relative income poverty in 2001 using three different sets of equivalence scale. Scale A is the 'national' scale most commonly used in the analysis of poverty in Ireland and which was derived from the relationship of social welfare rates for adults, qualified adults and child income support as they existed in the mid and late 1980s. Scale B has been widely used in the analysis of poverty and income distribution in the UK. Scale C, known as the OECD scale, was widely used in the analysis of poverty by the OECD and at EU level in the 1990s. It has been largely superseded in recent years by the OECD modified scale, which is now used by Eurostat to produce relative income poverty rates for Ireland. Figures using both the national scale and the OECD modified scale appear in the EU-SILC statistical release. The key observation from Table 9.4 is that the use of different equivalence scales makes little difference to overall rates of relative income poverty at the 50 per cent, 60 per cent and 70 per cent levels.

The use of multiple equivalence scales has been endorsed by researchers in the field. For example, Conniffe *et al.* (1998) point out that it is common

Table 9.4: *Relative income poverty using different equivalence scales, 2001*

	Scale A (1.0/0.66/0.33) (%)	Scale B (1.0/0.6/0.4) (%)	Scale C (1.0/0.7/0.5) (%)
50% median income line	12.9	14.6	12.9
60% median income line	21.9	21.9	21.5
70% median income line	29.3	30.0	30.1

Source: Whelan *et al.* (2003)

practice in research on poverty and income distribution internationally to use a number of scales because the uncertainties about which method produces the most satisfactory results mean that one cannot rely too heavily on any particular set of scales. However, as with the median/mean issue discussed above, the use of multiple equivalence scales in the dissemination of poverty data and in studies and research in this area results in multiple figures being quoted for the headline, or overall, rate of poverty, all of which are technically correct.

Household versus individual
Another source of confusion stems from whether it is the household or the individual person that is the focus of the analysis. Whelan *et al.* (2003) suggest that, while the position of households is relevant, the central underlying concern is about how individuals are affected by poverty. Reflecting this, it is now common practice in Ireland and at EU level to focus on the proportion of persons rather than households below poverty thresholds.

However, changing the focus from the household to the person has implications for the way relative income poverty thresholds are calculated. For example, in the case of mean-based thresholds, equivalent income is averaged across households to produce household-based figures. To obtain figures for individuals, the equivalised income of the household is first attributed to each member and then income is averaged over all individuals. Applying both approaches to data from the LIIS, Nolan *et al.* (2002) and Whelan *et al.* (2003) find that averaging equivalent income across individuals as opposed to households produces different figures for mean, or average, equivalent income. Where poverty thresholds are calculated as a fixed percentage of the mean, therefore, these will also differ as a consequence, as will the poverty rates obtained.

Table 9.5 illustrates the implications for poverty rates associated with changing the unit of analysis from household to individual or vice versa. It shows that there are slight differences in the rates of consistent poverty at the 40 per cent and 60 per cent of mean income thresholds. The differences in the rates of relative income poverty, however, are more pronounced. The proportion of households falling below the 50 per cent of mean income threshold, for example, was 23.8 per cent in 2001, whereas the proportion of persons falling below that threshold was somewhat lower at 18.4 per cent.

Table 9.5: *Mean-based poverty rates for households and individuals, 2001*

	Relative income poverty (%)	Consistent poverty (%)
Households		
Proportion below 40% of mean income	9.8	2.5
Proportion below 50% of mean income	23.8	4.1
Proportion below 60% of mean income	32.2	5.2
Persons		
Proportion below 40% of mean income	8.1	2.9
Proportion below 50% of mean income	18.4	4.1
Proportion below 60% of mean income	27.5	4.9

Source: Whelan *et al.* (2003)

Atkinson *et al.* (2002) point out that a change in focus from the household to the individual also has implications for poverty analysis based on median income. This is because the median obtained using the distribution of adult equivalised income among individuals will typically differ from the median of the distribution among households.

One of the main difficulties arises when analysing the evolution of poverty over time. Here, Nolan *et al.* (2000) point out that much of the early research on the Irish income distribution refers to the distribution among households. It is only on that basis, for example, that results are available from the 1973 and 1980 Household Budget Surveys. This obliges researchers and analysts to deal with the distribution among households at some points and the distribution among persons at other points, which has clear implications for comparability in longitudinal analyses.

Collection of income data and different definitions of income

Differences in the way income is collected and measured can also impact on measured poverty. Nolan *et al.* (2000) note the different methods of measuring income data in the Living in Ireland Survey (LIIS) and the Household Budget Survey (HBS) compared to the European Community Household Panel (ECHP). The LIIS and HBS recorded details for most sources of income in respect of the amount received in the 'current' pay period (week, fortnight and month) with longer periods taken for certain other income sources (self-employment, farming and so on), whereas the ECHP adopted an annual accounting period with an income figure collected which related to the previous calendar year. Clearly, the figures obtained from the 'current' period may differ from those relating to the previous calendar year.

Table 9.6 shows the distribution of income based on the 'current' method of collection under the LIIS in 1994 and the annual method for the 1994 ECHP. The 1994 ECHP was based on 1993 income data (the previous calendar year). Here we see that the two different methods give rise to slight differences at all decile points in the income distribution. The top decile in particular records a marked change, accounting for 26.4 per cent of total income under the 'current' measure but 28.3 per cent under the annual measure. This higher share for the top decile under the annual measure is offset, however, by lower corresponding shares for the other deciles in the top half of the income distribution.

Table 9.6: *Distribution of disposable income among Irish households, current (LIIS) versus annual (ECHP) income, 1994*

Income decile	% share in total disposable income	
	Current	Annual
Bottom	2.3	2.2
2nd	3.3	3.2
3rd	4.6	4.5
4th	6.0	5.8
5th	7.5	7.3
6th	9.1	8.8
7th	11.1	10.7
8th	13.5	13.0
9th	16.5	16.2
Top	26.4	28.3

Source: Nolan *et al.* (2000)

Income is defined differently in Ireland than it is at EU level, with the differences centring on the treatment of pensions (see Chapter 2). Table 9.7 shows that the use of two income definitions results in two quite different sets of income figures. For example, the national figure for average disposable household income is somewhat higher than the corresponding EU figure. In contrast, the national figure for median income and the 60 per cent median income threshold are lower than the corresponding EU figures. Although it must be borne in mind that part of the difference is accounted for by the use of different equivalence scales.

Table 9.7: *Differences between national and EU income measures,* 2004*

| | National | | EU | |
	Annual (€)	Weekly (€)	Annual (€)	Weekly (€)
Average disposable household income	38,631	740.35	37,504	718.75
Average equivalised disposable household income	18,773	359.78	20,666	396.05
Median income	16,133	310.25	17,942	345.04
60% median income poverty threshold	9,680	185.51	10,765	206.30

* National equivalised values are obtained using the national scale (1.0/0.66/0.33); EU equivalised values are obtained using the OECD modified scale (1.0/0.5/0.3)
Source: CSO (2005b)

Not surprisingly, the differences recorded in Table 9.7, in particular for median income and the 60 per cent of median income threshold, result in two sets of relative income poverty rates: a national rate and an EU rate. Table 9.8 shows how the proportion of people below relative income thresholds in 2003 and 2004 differs when national and EU definitions of income and equivalence scales are applied. In all but one case (the proportion of persons below 70 per cent of median income in 2003), the EU rates of relative income poverty are higher than the national rates. Significantly, particularly from a policy-making perspective, EU and national rates show different trends. For example, focusing on the key 60 per cent of median income threshold, we see a slight fall in the national rate of poverty from 2003 to 2004 from 19.7 per cent to 19.4 per cent, whereas the EU figures show that relative income poverty is rising, up from 20.1 per cent in 2003 to 20.9 per cent in 2004.

Table 9.8: *Persons below national and EU relative income poverty thresholds,* 2004*

| | 2003 | | 2004 | |
	National (%)	EU (%)	National (%)	EU (%)
Below 50% of median income	11.6	12.3	11.1	11.4
Below 60% of median income	19.7	20.1	19.4	20.9
Below 70% of median income	27.7	27.0	28.7	29.0

* National equivalised values are obtained using the national scale (1.0/0.66/0.33); EU equivalised values are obtained using the OECD modified scale (1.0/0.5/0.3)
Source: CSO (2005b)

Therefore, differences in the way that income is collected, measured and defined can result in different sets of poverty figures and, in some cases, different poverty trends.

Addressing this difficulty

Unlike previous chapters, there is no clear approach to addressing this difficulty that lends itself to detailed exploration here. However, there are a number of important conclusions and policy suggestions which can be drawn from the preceding analysis and which can inform Ireland's future approach to the selection of poverty indicators, their use and how they are communicated. These conclusions and suggestions are dealt with below.

Conclusions and implications

This chapter explored a number of issues which together go some way towards explaining the communication and assimilation difficulties associated with the way poverty is currently measured in Ireland.

The use of two headline measures of poverty – relative income poverty and consistent poverty – contributes to a sense of confusion in relation to how many people are poor and who the poor are. Reflecting its multi-dimensional character, the ESRI has consistently argued that more than one measure is required in order to gain a fuller picture of poverty (Layte *et al.*, 2001a; Maître *et al.*, 2006). However, both measures are widely used and have produced, during the 1990s in particular, clearly conflicting poverty trends and indications as to who is poor. Therefore, the benefits obtained by using more than one measure in terms of a more comprehensive account of poverty need to be balanced against the costs in terms of the confusion and misunderstanding which can result.

Significant revisions to data impact on the credibility of the measures and undermine their public acceptability. The 2003 EU-SILC results originally showed a continuing rise in relative income poverty rates from 2001 to 2003 – up from 21.9 per cent to 22.7 per cent – but this was subsequently revised downwards by three percentage points to 19.7 per cent, reversing the previously rising poverty trend in the process. The revisions also resulted in notable changes at the disaggregated level and also to other indicators such as the summary measures of income inequality (Gini coefficient and the quintile share ratio). Although inevitable to some extent, such data revisions need to be avoided wherever possible. The challenge, which statistical organisations such as the CSO are conscious of, is to balance the need for ever more timely data with the need to produce accurate and definitive statistics.

Further difficulties are posed by the selective use of statistics by individuals or organisations to best support the case being made. There is scope for playing up the incidence and gravity of poverty and, equally, for suggesting that poverty is being addressed. Such manipulation of data is inevitable and probably unavoidable. It is, however, important to acknowledge that it is a factor which contributes to the public's confusion about poverty, as is the related problem of unintended misuse of statistics arising from poor understanding of how poverty is measured.

This chapter also noted that very different but equally legitimate figures could be produced using different methodologies. Examples include the use of the mean instead of the median, the national equivalence scale instead of the modified OECD scale, the EU definition of income instead of the national definition of income and focusing on the household as opposed to the individual. The result is that four people could come up with four somewhat different relative income poverty rates using a 60 per cent threshold and all four figures could be technically correct. Therefore, depending on which report or study you read, the figure quoted for relative income poverty, for example, at the headline or disaggregated level, may vary. These varying figures tend to be quoted in newspaper or journal articles about poverty. As well as giving rise to confusion and misunderstanding, such variations have a damaging impact on the credibility of the system of measures in that the public may end up wondering which is the 'right' figure or indeed, whether any of the figures are 'right'.

In view of these issues, there is a role for the government to seek to promote a methodologically coherent and streamlined approach to the way poverty is measured in Ireland. It is clear that there is a need to be consistent with international best practice in terms of the way these measures are calculated. For example, if the national approach to the calculation of relative income poverty was brought fully into line with the EU approach as set out in the Laeken indicators, then there would no longer be a need for the use of a national equivalence scale or national definitions of income. The EU-SILC, instead of producing a national and an EU figure, would produce a single figure for relative income poverty. This approach would reduce the number of different figures for poverty being produced by different means, thereby reducing the potential for confusion and assisting more effective communication.

The overall conclusion from the preceding analysis is that there is a need to promote a better and wider understanding of the way we measure poverty and why. This involves communicating poverty data more effectively and to as wide an audience as possible. A communications strategy would seek to promote a better understanding of the measures which are currently used, why they are used, how they are calculated and the limitations associated with them. Ultimately the value of the system of measures we adopt, not only depends on issues such as timeliness and accuracy but also on the extent to which they are understood and accepted by the users of the data: policy-makers and the public at large.

10

Conclusions

Poverty is a controversial issue, with no agreed definition or politically neutral standpoint. When it comes to measuring poverty, the literature affirms the predominance of financial measures, using income as the key indicator, and draws attention to their limitations as robust and objective measures of poverty.

This study set out to analyse six difficulties associated with the two key measures of poverty in Ireland: relative income poverty and the combined income and deprivation measure known as consistent poverty. It also aimed to illuminate the scope for addressing these difficulties.

Chapter 4 considered the difficulty posed by the paradox of high economic growth and high relative income poverty rates in Ireland in recent years and its implications for the credibility of relative income poverty measures. The analysis concluded that this has come about as the result of the interplay of a range of causal factors, including:

- Growth in earnings which outpaced inflation
- Growth in disposable income which outpaced earnings growth, particularly in the middle and at the higher end of the income distribution
- Demographic and structural trends which resulted, *inter alia*, in a reduction in the average equivalised household size
- Labour market trends in terms of the rise in the number of dual income households
- Increases in social welfare rates which, although substantial in real terms, failed to keep pace with the disposable income growth at the middle of the income distribution fuelled by the tax reforms of the late 1990s
- Levels of social expenditure which have been lower than the EU average, even when demographic and other factors such as unemployment are taken into account.

The number and complexity of the factors involved means that there is no easy way to address this paradox. However, an important first step from the perspective of the policy-maker is to understand these factors and how they interact to produce the rates of poverty seen in Ireland in recent years. There is also a clear challenge in terms of communicating and explaining the reasons for the paradox of high poverty and high economic growth to the general public. The approach taken in the UN's *Human Development Report 2005*, which included, for the first time, an explanatory box entitled 'The Two Tales of Irish Poverty', provides a pointer in that regard.

In an important finding, the analysis in Chapter 4 did suggest, however, that the rise in relative income poverty rates since the late 1990s could be reversed in the coming years because of a number of moderating factors. First, Budgets 2005, 2006 and 2007 introduced significant increases to social welfare rates. Second, the tax reforms which benefited primarily the middle classes with a tax liability have, for the moment, come to an end. Overall budgetary policy has become distinctly progressive in recent years with the ESRI estimating that Budgets 2005 and 2006 could reduce relative income poverty by 0.5 per cent and 0.4 per cent respectively (Callan *et al.*, 2004b and 2006).

Another significant finding relates to the proportion of those below the poverty line who are students. The analysis argued that students in higher education are a somewhat unique category as their spell in poverty is expected to be transitory: their earnings capacity is limited during full-time study but they are expected, on graduation, to be in a position to secure employment that will take them above the poverty line. If students in higher education were excluded from the analysis, the poverty rate would fall by 1.05 per cent.

Chapter 5 explored the problem of cross-country comparisons of relative income poverty rates giving misleading impressions as to the wellbeing of one country versus another. When such comparisons show economically less-developed countries achieving better rankings than richer countries, the public acceptability of relative income measures is damaged. The analysis showed that to make such comparisons, however, is not to compare like with like. For example, Eurostat figures for 2003 show that Ireland had the second highest rate of poverty in the EU-25 at 20 per cent. Hungary, by contrast, had one of the lowest poverty rates at 12 per cent. Comparisons of these rates are not based around any common standard or threshold of poverty so that to compare 'national' relative income poverty rates between Ireland and Hungary is to compare Irish poverty with Hungarian poverty. The difficulty posed by comparing 'national' rates of poverty in this way is that they imply to the general public that there are more poor people in Ireland than in Hungary – a country that is considerably less affluent.

The use of indicators with a national frame of reference had limited practical consequences when the median income gaps between EU countries were narrow, however it has become a particular issue since recent EU enlargements widened the gap between the poorest and richest member states. It was argued that, while the conceptualisation and measurement of poverty with reference to nationally defined income thresholds is certainly useful in a national context and for the purposes of informing policy-making at national level, it has become inadequate at EU level in a post-enlargement context.

To make meaningful comparisons in a European context requires a consensus on what it is to be poor in a European context. The analysis therefore considered the merits of a measure of EU-wide relative income poverty. Such an approach uses the EU, as opposed to the member state, as the frame of reference and sets a 60 per cent of median income threshold for the EU as a whole, calculating the percentage of the population in each member state falling below the threshold. Under such a measure, Ireland is transformed from one of the worst performers on the basis of a straight comparison of national poverty rates to one of the best. Unlike a comparison of national poverty rates, this measure would quite rightly suggest to the data user that Ireland is better off than Hungary.

As poverty is defined nationally – and because people are considered to be in poverty, disadvantaged or excluded relative to the immediate society in which they live – national poverty rates should remain the primary focus. However, there is scope for the introduction of an EU-wide measure of relative income poverty as a secondary Laeken indicator to complement existing national indicators and to facilitate a more meaningful comparative analysis of poverty in an EU context. It could also serve as a useful measure of future European integration.

Chapter 6 addressed the difficulty stemming from the fact that income data does not capture everything about the needs of an individual or household. This situation has particular implications for the validity of relative income poverty trends for certain groups in society such as those dependent on social welfare. These groups benefit from a range of state services and supports that are not traditionally counted as part of the relative income poverty measure. Yet during the 1990s, this measure showed increasing proportions of vulnerable groups such as lone parents, the ill/disabled, the elderly and the unemployed falling into poverty.

To gain a more rounded view of the position of these groups, Chapter 6 first explored a 'direct' approach to the monetary valuation of public services and in-kind benefits. The analysis highlighted the difficulties associated with estimating the value of public services to such vulnerable groups. For example, to adopt fully such a direct approach would involve an onerous survey process to audit public service usage before attempting to assign valuations to households which could then be factored into the analysis of income. However, in view of the scale of the resources committed to the provision of public services, further work could usefully be done to establish the scope for gathering the necessary data in a cost-effective way.

In terms of in-kind benefits, the analysis shows that the Household Benefits Package and fuel allowances are worth up to €1,309.20 per year or €25.18 per week to recipients, who are primarily elderly. Since the introduction of the EU-SILC, these in-kind benefits have been included in the analysis of income. A breakdown of EU-SILC data shows that their inclusion results in a drop in the relative income poverty rate by two percentage points. At the disaggregated level in particular, the inclusion of the in-kind benefits has the effect of reducing poverty levels for a number of social welfare groups who receive these benefits, most notably the retired. This finding provides evidence of the effectiveness of public expenditure on in-kind benefits in terms of improving the circumstances of those on the lowest incomes and of reducing poverty.

However, placing values on a number of other important in-kind benefits that make a difference to the living standards and quality of life of those on low incomes continues to present considerable conceptual and methodological problems. Examples include the free travel pass and the medical card, which are still not taken into account in the analysis of income and the calculation of poverty rates. Given these difficulties, it is clear that the relative income poverty measure does not provide a full picture of the situation of those on low incomes who receive a range of state benefits and supports. As such, the validity and value of relative income poverty data to the policy-maker can be legitimately questioned.

This finding prompted consideration of an alternative 'indirect' approach to addressing the difficulty posed by the need to incorporate state services, in-kind benefits and supports into the measurement of poverty. The budget standards approach avoids the problems associated with estimating the value of benefits such as the medical card and the free travel pass. It effectively incorporates the value of such subsidies into the analysis because the income required to achieve a basic standard of living by a given household which receives these benefits will be lower than the income required by a similar household that has to pay for these services. Analysis highlighted how, in 2004, a lone parent with two children and an unemployed couple with two children did not receive sufficient weekly income from the state to meet the expenditure required to achieve a 'low cost but acceptable' (LCA) standard of living, whereas a pensioner couple with no car enjoyed a modest weekly income surplus.

Chapter 6 then compared LCA budgets with the relative income poverty thresholds for different household types, including a provision for unexpected expenditure of €30 per week. This analysis found that the poverty threshold continued to exceed the income required for each of the budgets, with the exception of car-owning pensioners who require an income that is slightly higher than the threshold to be sure of a low cost but acceptable living standard. This finding reinforces the assertion that relative income poverty thresholds do not necessarily bear any explicit relationship to the income level that is required by households to achieve a certain standard of living.

When all in-kind benefits and other state supports are factored into the analysis, as with the budget standards approach, certain social welfare households can achieve an acceptable standard of living on an income that is below the poverty threshold. This analysis suggests that the relative income poverty measure may be overstating poverty in Ireland, particularly for key social welfare groups such as the elderly. It supports the assertion that poverty thresholds framed around the objectively defined needs set out in budget standards for selected vulnerable household types may be more meaningful to the policy-maker and may resonate more closely with the public. For example, if a household has an income less than the amount required for that household type to achieve a low cost but acceptable standard of living, then that household could reasonably be assumed to be living in poverty.

There is a case for examining the potential of mainstreaming a limited budget standards exercise in respect of selected vulnerable household types in Ireland. This could inform policy on rates of social welfare and child income support. It would also provide a means of tracking the benefit of services to these vulnerable groups. Such budgets could be uprated annually to reflect changes in the Consumer Price Index and reformulated periodically, for example every five years to coincide with the rebasing of the Consumer Price Index.

Chapter 7 set out to examine the fact that the relative income poverty measure also fails to take account of housing expenditure or the benefits of outright ownership of housing and the reduced rent paid by those in local authority accommodation. This is particularly significant in an Irish context, where average house prices and rents in the private sector have soared in recent years, while the costs of accommodation rented from local authorities have remained stable. In addition, almost half of all dwellings in the state are owned outright, predominantly by older age groups, and consequently such households do not incur mortgage or rent-related housing expenditure.

The analysis considered two possible approaches aimed at addressing this difficulty. The first is the housing expenditures approach, as used in the UK, which aims to adjust household income in order to 'correct' for differences in the levels of housing expenditure across households. Applied in an Irish context, it leads to a marginal (0.8 per cent) fall in the overall relative income poverty rate due to offsetting effects. At the disaggregated level, poverty rates fall for outright owners, social renters, the retired and farmers, and rise for private renters, mortgage-holders, the employed and the self-employed. The housing expenditures approach provides a different but not necessarily a better account of a household's command over resources. Were such an approach to be adopted in Ireland, it would be prudent to present figures on both bases on the grounds that the truth probably lies somewhere in between.

In contrast to the housing expenditures approach, the imputed rent approach is concerned with the benefit of housing costs saved by people who own their homes outright or who are paying subsidised rents. Again, this approach improves the relative position of outright homeowners and in particular the wellbeing of the elderly. This finding has implications for the position of the retired as presented in poverty statistics, as the incorporation of imputed rent could significantly improve the relative position of, and reduce poverty rates for, the retired population sub-group in Ireland. There is a clear link here to the conclusions reached in Chapter 6 in relation to the implications of the inclusion of state supports and in-kind benefits on poverty rates for older people.

Although the housing expenditures approach and the imputed rent approach are effective ways of dealing with the housing issue in the measurement and analysis of poverty, they are not without their problems, criticisms and shortcomings. These need to be considered more fully in the context of any evaluation or assessment of their utility and applicability in an Irish context. Other possibilities for incorporating housing into the analysis of poverty and social exclusion also merit further investigation. For example, Atkinson et al. (2005) recommend that thought should be given to devising a measure to identify those seriously at risk of poverty/exclusion due to housing costs.

Chapter 8 focused on the consistent poverty measure, which uses both an income threshold and a deprivation index to identify those in poverty. Many would argue that the credibility of this measure, around which Ireland's global poverty reducing target is currently framed, has been damaged following the conflicting trends that emerged as a result of the change from the LIIS to the EU-SILC. The analysis considered whether the consistent poverty measure adequately reflects the nature of poverty in contemporary Ireland, where society and living standards have changed considerably since the measure was first devised in 1987. Specifically, it could be argued that many of the deprivation items used in the measure relate to a more frugal era and that, therefore, it is an outdated concept of poverty that is being measured. This raises legitimate questions as to the extent to which such a measure continues to be meaningful from a policy-making perspective. The ESRI has made it clear that the consistent poverty measure was never intended to become an 'absolute' measure of poverty.

The issue centres on the relevance of indicators year on year. The analysis focused on the approach taken in successive studies of deprivation in the UK. Following the initial 1983 Breadline Britain Survey each of the two successive surveys (1990 and 1999) revisited the list of deprivation items, removing redundant items and/or adding new items. Many of the items added reflect the increasing importance of participation in social customs to people's quality of life and wellbeing. A preliminary survey is then undertaken using the new list to establish those items which a majority of the population regard as necessities. The evolution in the lists of deprivation items in these UK studies highlights the changing nature of deprivation over time. It demonstrates the need to revisit regularly the way we measure deprivation and to update deprivation questions in light of changes in living standards and societal expectations. The UK studies also demonstrate how this might be done.

A rebasing of the consistent poverty measure using an updated list of deprivation items at regular intervals, perhaps every five years in line with the rebasing of the Consumer Price Index, would help to maximise the validity and relevance of the measure in the eyes of the public. It would also ensure that consistent poverty continues to be a meaningful source of evidence-based information for the policy-maker.

Chapter 9 explored how the current system of measuring poverty has contributed to public confusion about how many people in Ireland are poor and who those people are. The analysis focused on the ways in which the measures are used and communicated.

First, the use of two headline measures of poverty – relative income poverty and consistent poverty – might be contributing to a general sense of confusion about the incidence of poverty in Ireland. During the 1990s, for example, they produced clearly conflicting poverty trends. At the disaggregated level, they continue to give a conflicting picture as to who is poor. It is clear that the benefits obtained by using more than one measure in terms of a more comprehensive account of the multi-dimensional nature of poverty need to be balanced against the costs in terms of the confusion and misunderstanding that can result.

Second, significant revisions to data damage the credibility of the measures and their public acceptability and need to be avoided to the greatest extent possible.

Third, the judicious use of statistics by individuals or organisations to support the particular case they wish to make also acts to obscure clarity and understanding. It is possible to 'play up' the incidence and gravity of poverty and, equally, to suggest that poverty is being addressed. Such manipulation of data is inevitable and probably unavoidable. It is important, however, to acknowledge that it contributes to the level of public confusion about poverty, as does the related problem of unintended misuse of statistics arising from poor understanding of how poverty is measured.

Fourth, different methodologies produce very different but equally legitimate figures. Examples include the use of the mean instead of the median, the national equivalence scale instead of the modified OECD scale, the household instead of the individual and the EU definition of income instead of the national definition of income. The result is that four people could come up with four somewhat different relative income poverty rates using a 60 per cent threshold and all four figures could be correct. As well as giving rise to confusion and misunderstanding, this situation damages the credibility of the system of measures in that the public ends up wondering which is the 'right' figure or indeed whether any of the figures are 'right'.

In view of these issues, there is a role for the government to promote a methodologically coherent and streamlined approach to the way poverty is measured in Ireland. It is clear that there is a need to be consistent with international best practice in terms of the way these measures are calculated. For example, if the national approach to the calculation of relative income poverty was to be brought fully into line with the EU approach, as set out in the Laeken indicators, then there would no longer be a need for the use of a national equivalence scale or a national definition of income. The EU-SILC, instead of producing a national and an EU figure for relative income poverty, would produce a single figure for this indicator. This approach would reduce the number of different figures for poverty being produced by different means, thereby lowering the potential for confusion and assisting more effective communication.

Ultimately, the value of the system of measures depends not only on issues such as timeliness and accuracy but also on the extent to which they are understood and accepted by the users of the data: policy-makers and the public at large. We need to promote a better and wider understanding of the way we measure poverty and why we measure it that way. This will involve communicating poverty data more effectively and to as wide an audience as possible. An appropriate communications strategy would seek to achieve a fuller understanding of the measures that are used, why they are used, how they are calculated and the limitations associated with them.

The concept of poverty itself is nebulous and the subject of continued debate in international literature. Not surprisingly, there continue to be differences of opinion in terms of how poverty should be measured. This prompted Atkinson (1987) to conclude that there is likely to be a diversity of judgements affecting all aspects of measuring poverty and that this should be recognised in the procedures adopted. The measures which have been adopted have their shortcomings and provide 'less all-embracing answers', but Atkinson argues that such 'partial answers' are better than no answer at all.

The analysis here suggests that the difficulties with relative income poverty measures are quite pronounced. Poverty is now widely conceptualised in terms of exclusion from the life of one's society because of lack of resources and involves experiencing various forms of what that particular society would regard as serious deprivation. However, relative income measures are limited in their ability to capture such exclusion. They do not take account of a number of significant factors that affect the standard of living of certain households. These include in-kind state benefits such as the free travel pass and the medical card and other subsidised state supports and services including housing. Consequently, the figures produced can provide a skewed picture of how many people are poor and who they are. Median income itself, on which such measures are based, is also subject to influence by a range of factors that cannot be controlled through social policy measures alone.

There are also shortcomings associated with Ireland's consistent poverty measure, which may be contributing to a loss of credibility for this measure. Yet there is scope for making it more publicly acceptable and relevant to contemporary Ireland.

An important issue worthy of further research relates to the distinction between the concepts of poverty and social exclusion. In seeking to modify the deprivation component of the consistent poverty measure, we need to consider carefully what exactly the indicator of consistent poverty is expected to measure. Should it seek to measure poverty in a strict sense or is it intended to encompass the broader concepts of social exclusion or even quality of life? In order to serve effectively as a means of measuring poverty, defined in relativist and participative terms, it must by necessity measure more than material hardship in the narrow sense. At the same time, in producing a broader measure of poverty one needs to have regard to the difficult distinction between poverty and social exclusion on the one hand and deficiencies in quality of life on the other. The latter, it is suggested, requires a different set of measures and forms part of a separate analysis.

The scale of these difficulties indicates that the search for satisfactory measures that guide policy in alleviating poverty is ongoing. In terms of setting future poverty reduction targets, the difficulties highlighted here raise questions about the value of focusing on rigid targets framed around either relative income poverty or consistent poverty. In this regard, the NESC (2005b) proposes that, while both measures produce a range of useful information, the effectiveness of anti-poverty strategies needs to be guided by diagnostic and performance indicators which focus specifically on policies and interventions and the outcomes that they are delivering for the most vulnerable groups in our society.

There remains no easy way to address the difficulties explored in this study. The research has pointed in the direction of a number of possible options through which the present system of poverty measurement in Ireland could usefully be enhanced and further developed. However, it has also highlighted the fact that such solutions generally raise further questions and present alternative challenges. From the policy-making perspective, the objective must be a more robust, reliable, publicly credible and acceptable set of measures capable of providing an effective basis for evidence-based social policy. It is hoped that this analysis will contribute to an informed consideration and discussion of how such measures may be achieved.

APPENDIX 1
The Laeken Indicators

Primary indicators
1 Low income rate after transfers with low income threshold set at 60 per cent of median income
2 Distribution of income (income quintile ratio)
3 Persistence of low income
4 Median low income gap
5 Regional cohesion
6 Long-term unemployment rate
7 People living in jobless households
8 Early school-leavers not in further education or training
9 Life expectancy at birth
10 Self-perceived health status

Secondary indicators
11 Dispersion around the 60 per cent of median low-income threshold
12 Low income rate anchored at a point in time
13 Low income rate before transfers
14 Distribution of income (Gini coefficient)
15 Persistence of low income (based on 50 per cent of median income)
16 Long-term unemployment share
17 Very long-term unemployment rate
18 Persons with low educational attainment

Source: EU Social Protection Committee, 'Report on Indicators in the Field of Poverty and Social Exclusion', October 2001: http://ue.eu.int/ueDocs/cms_Data/docs/pressData/en/misc/DOC.68841.pdf

APPENDIX 2
Topics in the LIIS Questionnaires

Household questionnaire
- Household size and composition
- Housing and physical environment
- Housing tenure
- Rent and mortgage payments
- Standard of living (things the household can afford to have or to do)
- Debts and arrears
- Sources of household income
- Non-cash and secondary benefits

Individual questionnaire
- Current activity status (self-defined)
- Detailed information on current job for those working fifteen or more hours per week in a job or business
- More limited information on work for those working less than fifteen hours per week
- Some information on previous job for those not currently working fifteen or more hours per week
- Job search activity for those seeking work
- Other daily activities such as caring responsibilities, social and political participation
- Recent involvement in education and training
- Activity in each month since the beginning of the previous calendar year
- Detailed information on income in the previous calendar year from employment, self-employment, personal and occupational pensions, social welfare, education/training-related allowances and grants, property (interest, dividends, rental income) and other sources
- Health status, health service usage and healthcare coverage
- General outlook on life

APPENDIX 3
Calculating the Value of the 'Free Schemes' (2005)

Telephone allowance
The telephone allowance scheme provides a payment towards a telephone bill. The value of the allowance is:
€40.82 plus VAT [€49.40 including VAT] if billed every two months
or
€20.41 plus VAT [€24.70 including VAT] if billed monthly
Annual value = €24.70 × 12 = €296.40

Free TV licence
Those who qualify for the Household Benefits Package are also entitled to a free television licence from its next renewal date.
Annual value = €155.00

Electricity/natural gas/bottled gas allowance
This allowance is made up of four different options. Those with an electricity and natural gas supply must select the electricity allowance or natural gas allowance. The electricity (group account) allowance is only available to persons who have an electricity slot meter or where the registered consumer of electricity is a landlord. The bottled gas refill allowance is only available to those who do not have an electricity or natural gas supply.

The electricity allowance covers normal standing charges and up to 1,800 units of electricity each year.

The natural gas allowance is an alternative to the electricity allowance if the home is connected to a natural gas supply. It covers normal standing or supply charges and a certain amount of natural gas kilowatt hours each year. The amount varies depending on the tariff.

Those living in self-contained accommodation (a flat or an apartment) who have an electricity slot meter or where the registered consumer of electricity at their address is a landlord may qualify for an electricity (group account) allowance. This is made up of a book of twelve vouchers that may be put towards electricity costs.

Those whose homes are not connected to an electricity or natural gas supply but otherwise satisfy the conditions of the scheme, may get the bottled gas refill allowance as an alternative. It is made up of a book of fifteen vouchers that may be exchanged for a cylinder of gas at retail outlets.

Calculation of value of the electricity allowance only
Standing charges:
Bi-monthly standing charge = €10.38 including VAT
    €10.38 × 6 = €62.28 per year
Public service obligation charge = €2.26 per month including VAT
    €2.26 × 12 = €27.12 per year
Entitlement of 1,800 free units
Day rate = €0.1385 per unit
    €0.1385 × 1,800 = €249.30
    Annual value = €62.28 + €27.12 + €249.30 = €338.70

Fuel allowance
The national fuel scheme is intended to help households who are dependent on long-term social welfare or Health Service Executive payments and who are unable to provide for their own heating needs. The scheme operates for twenty-nine weeks from the end of September to mid-April.
    Rate of payment = €14 per week
    Annual value = €14 × 29 = €406 (2006)

Smokeless fuel allowance
The smokeless fuel allowance is paid by the Department of Social and Family Affairs to low-income households in Ireland to help them meet the extra costs of using smokeless or low-smoke fuels in certain parts of the country.
    Rate of payment = €3.90 per week
    Annual value = €3.90 × 29 = €113.10
    Combined annual value of fuel allowances = €519.10

Sources: Department of Social and Family Affairs booklet SW107 and www.oasis.gov.ie

References

Atkinson, A. B. (1974), 'Poverty and Income Inequality in Britain', in Wedderburn, D. (ed.), *Poverty, Inequality and Class Structure*, Cambridge University Press

Atkinson, A. B. (1987), 'On the Measurement of Poverty', *Econometrica*, vol. 55, no. 4, pp. 749–764

Atkinson, A. B. (1998), *Poverty in Europe*, Blackwell Publishers

Atkinson, A. B. (2003), 'Social Europe and Social Science', *Social Policy & Society*, vol. 2, no. 4, pp. 261–272

Atkinson, A. B., Cantillon, B., Marlier, E. and Nolan, B. (2002), *Social Indicators – The EU and Social Inclusion*, Oxford University Press

Atkinson, A. B., Cantillon, B., Marlier, E. and Nolan, B. (2005), *Taking Forward the EU Social Inclusion Process – Report (Final Version Dated 31 July 2005) – An Independent Report Commissioned by the Luxembourg Presidency of the Council of the European Union*, Le Gouvernement Du Grand Duché De Luxembourg – Ministère de la Famille et de l'Intégration

Benchmarking and Indexation Group (2001), 'Final Report of the Social Welfare Benchmarking and Indexation Group', report of a social partnership working group under the Programme for Prosperity and Fairness

Beveridge, W. (1942), *Social Insurance and Allied Services (Report by Sir William Beveridge)*, HMSO

Bradshaw, J. (1993), *Budget Standards for the United Kingdom*, Joseph Rowntree Foundation, Ashgate Publishing

Bradshaw, J. (2004), 'Foreword', in MacMahon, B., Delaney, M. and Feely, N., *Low Cost But Acceptable Budgets for Three Households,* Vincentian Partnership for Social Justice

Bramley, G. (1997), 'Poverty and Local Public Services', in Gordon, D. and Pantazis, C. (eds.), *Breadline Britain in the 1990s*, Joseph Rowntree Foundation

Calandrino, M. (2003), *Low Income and Deprivation in British Families – An Exploratory Analysis of the 'Consistent Poverty' Approach to Poverty Measurement Using Data for Great Britain Drawn from the Families and Children Study*, Department of Work and Pensions

Callan, T., Keeney, M., Nolan, B. and Maître, B. (2004a), *Why is Relative Income Poverty so High in Ireland?*, ESRI

Callan, T., Nolan, B. and Whelan, C. T. (1993), 'Resources, Deprivation and the Measurement of Poverty', *Journal of Social Policy*, vol. 22, no. 2, pp. 141–172

Callan, T., Walsh, J. and Coleman, K. (2004b), 'Budget 2005: Impact on Income Distribution and Relative Income Poverty', *ESRI Quarterly Economic Commentary*, Winter

Callan, T., Walsh, J. and Coleman, K. (2006), 'Budget 2006: Impact on Income Distribution and Relative Income Poverty', *ESRI Quarterly Economic Commentary*, Spring

Cantillon, S. (2000), 'Equality in Economic and Other Dimensions', in O'Hagan, J. (ed.), *The Economy of Ireland: Policy and Performance of a European Region*, Gill & Macmillan

Central Statistics Office (2003), *House Prices and the Consumer Price Index – Explanatory Note*, Central Statistics Office

Central Statistics Office (2005a), *EU Survey on Income and Living Conditions* (EU-SILC) *2003*, Stationery Office

Central Statistics Office (2005b), *EU Survey on Income and Living Conditions (EU-SILC) 2004 (with revised 2003 estimates)*, Stationery Office

Central Statistics Office (2005c), *Measuring Ireland's Progress 2004*, Stationery Office

Central Statistics Office (2005d), *Statistical Yearbook of Ireland 2005*, Stationery Office

Collins, M. L. (2004), 'Urban Deprivation: The Experience of a Dublin Community', in Drudy, P. J. and MacLaran, A. (eds.), *Dublin: Economic and Social Trends*, vol. 4, Centre for Urban and Regional Studies, Trinity College Dublin

Commission of the European Communities (1981), *Final Report from the Commission to the Council on the First Programme of Pilot Schemes and Studies to Combat Poverty*, Commission of the European Communities

Commission on Social Welfare (1986), *Report of the Commission on Social Welfare*, Stationery Office

Conniffe, D., Nolan, B. and Whelan, C. T. (1998), *Household Composition, Living Standards and 'Needs' – Final Report for the Working Group Examining the Treatment of Married, Cohabiting and One-Parent Households Under the Tax and Social Welfare Codes*, ESRI

Corrigan, C., Fitzgerald, E., Bates, J. and Matthews, A. (2002), *Data Sources on Poverty*, Institute of Public Administration

Department of Finance (2003), *Budget 2004*, Government of Ireland

Department of Work and Pensions (2003), *Measuring Child Poverty*, HMSO

Department of Work and Pensions (2005), *Households Below Average Income 2003/04*, HMSO

EEC (1984), 'On Specific Community Action to Combat Poverty, Council Decision of 19 December 1984, 85/8/EEC', *Official Journal of the EEC*, vol. 2, no. 24

European Commission (2004), *Joint Report on Social Inclusion 2004*, DG Employment and Social Affairs

Eurostat (1998), 'Recommendations on Social Exclusion and Poverty Statistics', 31st Meeting of the Statistical Programme Committee, Luxembourg, 26 and 27 November

Eurostat *(1999)*, *European Community Household Panel (ECHP): Selected Indicators from the 1995 Wave,* Office for Official Publications of the European Communities

Fahey, T. (2005), *The Case for an EU-wide Measure of Poverty*, Working Paper no. 169, ESRI

Fahey, T., Nolan, B. and Maître, B. (2004a), *Housing, Poverty and Wealth in Ireland*, Combat Poverty Agency

Fahey, T., Nolan, B. and Maître, B. (2004b), 'Housing Expenditures and Income Poverty in EU Countries', *Journal of Social Policy*, vol. 33, no. 3, pp. 437–454

Fahey, T., Whelan, C. T. and Maître, B. (2005), *First European Quality of Life Survey: Income Inequalities and Deprivation*, European Foundation for the Improvement of Living and Working Conditions

Frick, J. R. and Grabka, M. M. (2002), *The Personal Distribution of Income and Imputed Rent – A Cross-national Comparison for the UK, West Germany, and the USA*, German Institute for Economic Research

General Medical Services (Payments) Board (2004), *Report for the Year Ended 31st December 2003*, General Medical Services (Payments) Board

Gordon, D. (2000), 'Measuring Absolute and Overall Poverty', in Gordon, D. and Townsend, P. (eds.), *Breadline Europe: The Measurement of Poverty*, The Policy Press

Gordon, D. and Pantazis, C. (1997), *Breadline Britain in the 1990s*, Joseph Rowntree Foundation

Gordon, D., Adelman, L., Ashworth, K., Bradshaw, J., Levitas, R., Middleton, S., Pantazis, C., Patsios, D., Payne, S., Townsend, P. and Williams, J. (2000a), *Poverty and Social Exclusion in Britain*, Joseph Rowntree Foundation

Gordon, D., Pantazis, C. and Townsend, P. (2000b), 'Absolute and Overall Poverty: A European History and Proposal for Measurement', in Gordon, D. and Townsend, P. (eds.), *Breadline Europe: The Measurement of Poverty*, The Policy Press

Gordon, D., Pantazis, C. and Townsend, P. (2000c), *Changing Necessities of Life, 1983–1999, Poverty and Social Exclusion Survey of Britain*, Working Paper no. 3, Townsend Centre for International Poverty Research, University of Bristol

Halleröd, B., Bradshaw, J. and Holmes, H. (1997), 'Adapting the Consensual Definition of Poverty', in Gordon, D. and Pantazis, C. (eds.), *Breadline Britain in the 1990s*, Joseph Rowntree Foundation

Hills, J. (2004), *Inequality and the State*, Oxford University Press

Ireland (1997), *Sharing in Progress: National Anti-Poverty Strategy*, Stationery Office

Ireland (2001), *National Action Plan against Poverty and Social Exclusion 2001–2003*, Stationery Office

Ireland (2002), *Building an Inclusive Society: Review of the National Anti-Poverty Strategy under the Programme for Fairness and Prosperity*, Department of Social, Community and Family Affairs

Ireland (2003), *National Action Plan against Poverty and Social Exclusion 2003–2005*, Stationery Office

Ireland (2005), *Annual Housing Statistics Bulletin 2004*, Stationery Office

Ireland (2007), *National Action Plan for Social Inclusion 2007–2016*, Stationery Office

Lawlor, J. and McCarthy, C. (2003), 'Browsing Onwards: Irish Public Spending in Perspective', *Irish Banking Review*, Autumn

Layte, R., Maître, B., Nolan, B., Watson, D., Whelan, C. T., Williams, J. and Casey, B. (2001a), *Monitoring Poverty Trends and Exploring Poverty Dynamics in Ireland*, ESRI

Layte, R., Nolan, B. and Whelan, C. T. (2000), 'Targeting Poverty: Lessons from Monitoring Ireland's National Anti-Poverty Strategy', *Journal of Social Policy*, vol. 29, pp. 553–575

Layte, R., Nolan, B. and Whelan, C. T. (2001b), *The Changing Face of Poverty in Ireland*, ESRI

Layte, R., Nolan, B. and Whelan, C. T. (2004), 'Explaining Poverty Trends in Ireland during the Boom', *Irish Banking Review*, Summer

Mack, J. and Lansley, S. (1985), *Poor Britain*, Allen and Unwin

MacMahon, B., Delaney, M. and Feely, N. (2004), *Low Cost But Acceptable Budgets for Three Households,* Vincentian Partnership for Social Justice

Maître, B., Nolan, B. and Whelan, C. T. (2006), *Reconfiguring the Measurement of Deprivation and Consistent Poverty in Ireland*, ESRI

McKay, S. and Collard, S. (2004), *Developing Family Resources Survey Deprivation Questions*, Department of Work and Pensions

National Economic and Social Council (2005a), *The Developmental Welfare State,* Report no. 113, NESC

National Economic and Social Council (2005b), *NESC Strategy 2006: People, Productivity, Purpose*, Report no. 114, NESC

Nolan, B. (2001), 'Inequality: The Price of Prosperity?', *Studies – An Irish Quarterly Review*, vol. 90, no. 337, pp. 29–37

Nolan, B. (2002), 'Measuring and Targeting Poverty in Ireland', in Hauser, R. and Becker, I. (eds.), *Reporting on Income Distribution and Poverty – Perspectives from a German and a European Point of View*, Springer

Nolan, B. and Russell, H. (2001), *Non-Cash Benefits and Poverty in Ireland*, ESRI

Nolan, B. and Smeeding, T. (2004), *Ireland's Income Distribution in a Comparative Perspective*, Luxembourg Income Study

Nolan, B., Gannon, B., Layte, R., Watson, D., Whelan, C. T. and Williams, J. (2002), *Monitoring Poverty Trends in Ireland: Results from the 2000 Living in Ireland Survey*, ESRI

Nolan, B., Maître, B., O'Neill, D. and Sweetman, O. (2000), *The Distribution of Income in Ireland*, Oaktree Press

Nolan, B., Whelan, C. T. and Maître, B. (2005), 'Constructing Consistent Poverty Measures with EU-SILC Data: An Overview', unpublished working paper

O'Donnell, R. and Thomas, D. (1998), 'Partnership and Policy-making', in Healy, S. and Reynolds, B. (eds.), *Social Policy in Ireland: Principles, Practice and Problems*, Oaktree Press

Piachaud, D. (1987), 'Problems in the Definition and Measurement of Poverty', *Journal of Social Policy*, vol. 16, no. 2, pp. 147–164

Ringen, S. (1988), 'Direct and Indirect Measures of Poverty', *Journal of Social Policy*, vol. 17, no. 3, pp. 351–365

Rowntree, B. S. (1901), *Poverty: A Study of Town Life*, London: Macmillan

Russell, H., Layte, R., Maître, B., O'Connell, P. J. and Whelan, C. T. (2004), *Work Poor Households: The Welfare Implications of Changing Household Employment Patterns*, ESRI

Sen, A. K. (1982), *Poverty and Famines*, Oxford University Press

Social Protection Committee (2001), 'Report on Indicators in the Field of Poverty and Social Exclusion, October 2001', unpublished document

Social Protection Committee (2003), 'Mid Year Report from the Indicators Sub-Group to the Social Protection Committee – June 2003', unpublished document

Tovey, H., Haase, T. and Curtin, C. (1996), 'Understanding Rural Poverty', in Curtin, C., Haase, T. and Tovey, H. (eds.), *Poverty in Rural Ireland: A Political Economy Perspective*, Combat Poverty Agency Research Series, Oak Tree Press

Townsend, P. (1974), 'Poverty as Relative Deprivation: Resources and Style of Living', in Wedderburn, D. (ed.), *Poverty, Inequality and Class Structure*, Cambridge University Press

Townsend, P. (1979), *Poverty in the United Kingdom: A Survey of Household Resources and Standards of Living*, Penguin

Townsend, P. (1997), 'The Poverty Line: Methodology and International Comparisons', in Gordon, D. and Pantazis, C. (eds.), *Breadline Britain in the 1990s*, Joseph Rowntree Foundation

Townsend, P. and Gordon, D. (2002), 'Introduction', in Gordon, D., Adelman, L., Ashworth, K., Bradshaw, J., Levitas, R., Middleton, S., Pantazis, C., Patsios, D., Payne, S., Townsend, P. and Williams J. (eds.), *Poverty and Social Exclusion in Britain*, Joseph Rowntree Foundation

UNICEF (2000), 'A League Table of Child Poverty in Rich Nations', *Innocenti Report Card*, no. 1, June

United Nations (1995), *Report of the World Summit for Social Development*, Copenhagen, 6 to 12 March, UN

United Nations (2005), *Human Development Report 2005 – International Cooperation at a Crossroads – Aid, Trade and Security in an Unequal World*, UN Development Office

Whelan, C. T., Hannan, D. F. and Creighton, S. (1991), *Unemployment, Poverty and Psychological Distress*, General Research Series Paper no. 150, ESRI

Whelan, C. T., Layte, R., Maître, B., Gannon, B., Nolan, B., Watson, D. and Williams, J. (2003), *Monitoring Poverty Trends in Ireland: Results from the 2001 Living in Ireland Survey*, ESRI

Index